WATERFOWL HUNTING

© 1988 By National Rifle Association
Second Edition
reprint date February 2009

Produced by the NRA Hunter Services Department. For more information on the Hunter Skills Series, NRA Hunter Clinic Program, or becoming a volunteer hunter clinic instructor, contact NRA Hunter Services Department, 11250 Waples Mill Road, Fairfax, Virginia 22030. Telephone (703) 267-1516.

Library of Congress Catalog Card Number: 89122509

Main entry under title:
Waterfowl Hunting-NRA Hunter Skills Series

ISBN 978-0-935998-91-7

NR40835HR08690 (paperback)

ACKNOWLEDGEMENTS

Authors
Mike Strandlund, Editor, *Bowhunting World*
Matthew S. Fleming, Program Coordinator,
    NRA Hunter Services Department
Pat Nolan, Professional Retriever Trainer, Ponderosa Kennels
Jack Jagoda, Professional Retriever Trainer, Deep Run Farms
Don Zutz, Shotgun Shooting Columnist
Ed and Lue Park, Outdoor Writers and Photographers

Editors
Mike Strandlund, Editor, *Bowhunting World*
Matthew S. Fleming, Program Coordinator,
    NRA Hunter Services Department

Art
Doug Pifer, Former Resource Specialist,
    NRA Hunter Services Department

Co-Authors and Review Committee
Robert L. Davis, Jr., Manager, NRA Hunter Services
Gary L. Anderson, Former Executive Director, NRA General
    Operations
Jim Norine, Former Director, NRA Hunter Services
Dennis Eggers, Former South Central Regional Director,
    NRA Field Operations
Earl Hower, Former Program Manager, NRA Hunter Skills
Doug Pifer, Former Resource Specialist, NRA Hunter Services
Bill Lawton, Susquehanna River Waterfowlers Association
Eli Haydel, Haydel's Game Calls, Competitive
    Waterfowl Caller
Don Helmeke, Duckman Company, Waterfowl Conservationist
Keith Walters, Atlantic Flyway Editor, *Waterfowler's World*

Jeff Dershem, Susquehanna River Waterfowlers
Association
Ray Cachara, Susquehanna River Waterfowlers
Association
Dr. William Christy, Formerly of 4-H Shooting Sports,
Virginia Polytechnical Institute and State University
Ed Cornia, Former Hunter Education Coordinator, Utah
Division of Wildlife Resources
Jim Jones, U.S. Fish and Wildlife Service Federal Aid
Michael Berger, Former Director of Government Relations,
Ducks Unlimited
Wendell Carlson, Call-Maker, Carlson Custom Calls
Dahrl Wright, Call-Maker, Custom Calls

The National Rifle Association is grateful for the contributions
made by the preceding persons, by Ducks Unlimited, the Wildlife
Management Institute, and by the government agencies credited
throughout this book.

Photo Credits

Front cover photo by R. L. Davis, Jr.
Back cover photo by M. Fleming

NRA Hunter's Code of Ethics

I will consider myself an invited guest of the landowner, seeking his permission, and conduct myself that I may be welcome in the future.

I will obey the rules of safe gun handling and will courteously but firmly insist that others who hunt with me do the same.

I will obey all game laws and regulations, and will insist that my companions do likewise.

I will do my best to acquire marksmanship and hunting skills that assure clean, sportsmanlike kills.

I will support conservation efforts that assure good hunting for future generations of Americans.

I will pass along to younger hunters the attitudes and skills essential to a true outdoor sportsman.

NRA Gun Safety Rules

The fundamental NRA rules for safe gun handling are:

• **<u>ALWAYS</u> keep the gun pointed in a safe direction.**
• **<u>ALWAYS</u> keep your finger off the trigger until ready to shoot.**
• **<u>ALWAYS</u> keep the gun unloaded until ready to use.**

When using or storing a gun, always follow these NRA rules:

• **Know your target and what is beyond.**
• **Know how to use the gun safely.**
• **Be sure the gun is safe to operate.**
• **Use only the correct ammunition for your gun.**
• **Wear eye and ear protection as appropriate.**
• **Never use alcohol or drugs before or while shooting.**
• **Store guns so they are not accessible to unauthorized persons.**

Be aware that certain types of guns and many shooting activitiesrequire additional safety precautions.
To learn more about gun safety, enroll in an NRA hunter clinic or state hunter education class, or an NRA safety training or basic marksmanship course.

TODAY'S AMERICAN HUNTER

If you're a hunter, you're one of 15 million Americans who love the outdoors, have a close tie with traditions, and help conserve our natural resources. You know the thrill and beauty of a duck blind at dawn, a whitetail buck sneaking past your stand, a hot-headed, bugling bull elk. With your friends and forefathers you share the rich traditions of knowing wild places and good hunting dogs. Your woodsmanship and appreciation of nature provide food for body and soul.

And through contributions to hunting licenses and stamps, conservation tax funds, and sportsman clubs, you are partly responsible for the dramatic recovery of wildlife and its habitat. Hunters can take great pride—and satisfaction that only hunters know—in the great increases of deer, turkeys, elk, some waterfowl, and other species over the last century.

Your involvement with the National Rifle Association of America is also important to promote conservation and sportsmanship. In NRA, concerned hunters and shooters work together for laws and programs of benefit to the shooting sports. Most important is the education of sportsmen through programs like the nationwide Hunter Clinic Program operated by the NRA Hunter Services Department. Through the program and the Hunter Skills Series of how-to hunting books, America's already admirable hunters can keep improving their skills, safety, responsibility, and sportsmanship to help ensure our country's rich hunting traditions flourish forever.

Photo courtesy of Robert L. Davis, Jr.

CONTENTS Page

Photo courtesy of U.S. Fish and Wildlife Service

Photo courtesy of Jeff B. Johnston

Dead ducks and geese piled like cordwood are common elements in old-time photos of waterfowlers during the market-hunting era. The new generation of hunters is more aware of safety and the value of a single "trophy."

WELCOME TO WATERFOWLING

W aterfowling is an American tradition, a worldwide tradition. It helped feed our pioneers, was important for a growing economy, and still helps support poor families in some parts of the world.

But for most of us, waterfowling is a purely enjoyable sport and treasured tie with the outdoors. It's an exhilarating pastime that spices our lives and provides lingering memories of whistling wings, frosty mornings, the smell of gunpowder and wet retrievers. To many sportsmen, waterfowl hunting comes close to *the* reason for living.

The purpose of this book is to present a comprehensive collection of waterfowl hunting basics and a few advanced techniques so that more people can share the pleasures of duck and goose hunting. Getting a grasp on fundamentals, then working on the sport's finer points, is the key to waterfowling success.

The following chapters will cover such topics as waterfowl biology, jumpshooting and pothole hunting, decoy usage, calling techniques, safety measures, and the differences between lead and steel shot. This latter point is especially important, as steel shot is now being used for waterfowling in the U.S. It is vital for hunters to know the differing ballistic properties, pellet counts, and other characteristics of the two types of shotgun pellets. You simply cannot follow the same thinking for steel shot as you do for lead.

The topics of lead poisoning of waterfowl and the required use of steel shot are of concern to hunters and the National Rifle Association. The NRA supports continued study of the lead poisoning issue and believes steel shot regulations are acceptable only for waterfowl hunting in specific areas where lead poisoning of waterfowl has been scientifically documented—not for upland game or other shotgun hunting. The NRA has long endorsed the "hotspot" approach to federal steel shot regulations. Because of the increasing use of steel shot for waterfowl, the NRA recognizes the need for steel shot education among hunters.

Later in this book you'll also find information on hunting the individual waterfowl species, such as diving ducks, puddlers,

Canada geese, and the snow/blue species. All of this is intended to help hunters improve their chances and further appreciate the birds they hunt.

Some words must be said about sportsmanship and conservation, which are the keystones of future waterfowling. Long-since past are the days of market hunting and enormous game bags. The encroachment of civilization has reduced the amount of natural habitat available to waterfowl, taking with it the fabled clouds of ducks and geese that once blackened the skies at migration time. Perhaps the old-timers exaggerated some when they told their splendid tales of seemingly never-ending flights, but one thing is certain today: It's up to the hunters to conserve ducks, geese, and waterfowl hunting itself. Let common sense and a concern for the sport's ethics prevail, and you can enjoy waterfowling now while ensuring its future.

Welcome to the wonderful world of waterfowling!

Part I

Before the Hunt

Photo courtesy of M. Embrey

Photo courtesy of Robert L. Davis, Jr.

CHAPTER 1

WATERFOWL BIOLOGY, BEHAVIOR, AND IDENTIFICATION

T he days when a waterfowler could go out and merely hunt "ducks" and "geese" without regard to species and gender are gone. Today's waterfowlers can't simply count their limits of ducks and geese. They must be able to identify species and gender in flight. The point system, species management, and drakes-only regulations have made waterfowl identification the top priority of every waterfowler worthy of the name.

This should not be looked upon as a burden, but rather as an opportunity...a chance to learn more about those wondrous wanderers of far places whose secretive habits and mysterious migrations captivate man's imagination.

On the practical side, the hunter who can identify his quarry in the air and who knows the favored haunts and habits of his prey has a considerable edge over the hunter who is ill prepared. He knows where wood ducks are likely to be hiding during the midday lull. He knows where to collect a giant Canada goose before the snow geese arrive from the far North.

On the philosophical side, the sportsman who delves into the wonderful world of waterfowl will be rewarded with one of the finest of lifelong hobbies, adding immeasurably to his year-round enjoyment of waterfowling. A pair of binoculars, a reference book, and a field trip are all it takes to make the waterfowl season last from one autumn to the next.

The truly conscientious hunter takes advantage of every bit of information available on the game he pursues and, in the process, develops a deeper appreciation for the animal and his sport.

3

Photo courtesy of Pat Nolan

Canada geese mate for life, but if one of the pair is killed, the survivor finds a new mate, often only hours after reaching breeding grounds. Developing your knowledge of waterfowl natural history like this will increase your appreciation of duck and goose hunting.

Flyways

A basic understanding of waterfowl flyways and migration corridors is important in developing an appreciation for ducks and geese.

We have all known since childhood that ducks and geese fly south for the winter. The concept of four great flyways channeling four distinctly different groups of waterfowl from northern breeding grounds to southern wintering grounds was most likely our first tantalizing insight into this awesome phenomenon. But the flyway concept is seriously oversimplified.

The "Four Great Flyways" are actually units contrived for management purposes. Established in 1948, the Pacific, Central, Mississippi, and Atlantic flyways represent compromises between biological and administrative considerations. By dividing North America into four parts, biologists and game managers are better able to evaluate waterfowl populations and propose regulations that are in the best interest of the resource and the sport.

Migration Corridors

Several theories address how waterfowl can navigate vast distances to their breeding and wintering grounds. But until we can actually "ask" a pintail how it finds its way across the Pacific Ocean to winter in the Hawaiian Islands, or "ask" the snow goose how it can leave James Bay in northern Canada and fly nonstop to the Louisiana Gulf Coast, we really do not know for sure just how they do it. And just maybe the adventurer in us hopes it will forever remain a mystery.

It is believed that waterfowl use a combination of visual landmarks, stars, sun, and the earth's magnetic field to navigate. However they do it, there is an almost unerring accuracy and predictability to their travels. Their routes have been identified to the extent that we now know them as migration corridors.

Photo courtesy of M. Embrey

Information obtained by banding waterfowl has helped biologists understand waterfowl migrations, life cycles, and behavior. Funded mainly by hunters' purchases of duck stamps, banding has been an important conservation tool.

*Reprinted with permission by the Wildlife Management Institute,
from Ducks, Geese, and Swans of North America, 3rd edition.*

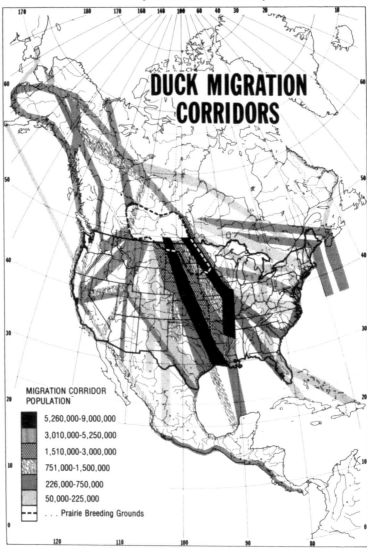

Radar tracking in the late 1950s and 1960s proved that ducks migrate east-west nearly as much as north-south. Heaviest movement is in the Central and Mississippi flyways.

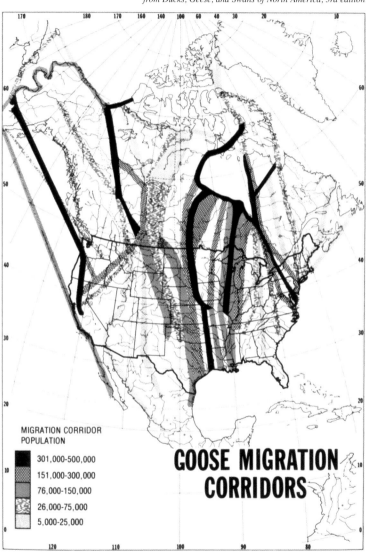

MIGRATION CORRIDOR
POPULATION

- 301,000-500,000
- 151,000-300,000
- 76,000-150,000
- 26,000-75,000
- 5,000-25,000

GOOSE MIGRATION CORRIDORS

Geese migrate greater distances than ducks in most cases, and are fairly evenly distributed across the flyways. Some geese, notably lesser snows, migrate at 50 miles per hour nonstop from their breeding to wintering grounds.

Reprinted with permission by the Wildlife Management Institute, from Ducks, Geese, and Swans of North America, 3rd edition.

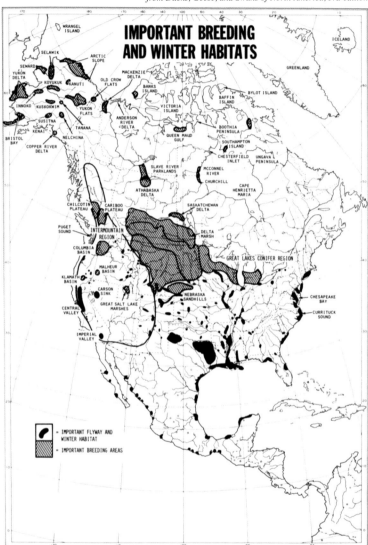

Favored waterfowl breeding areas are the prairie pothole region, an area of countless brood ponds, and the vast subarctic tundra regions that provide summer insect life to feed the young. The densest winter populations are along fertile coastal areas and major river systems of the mid-South.

Homing Instinct

While it is one thing to leave the northland autumn and head for more hospitable climes, it is yet another matter for a female wood duck to return to the exact duck house where she hatched a brood the previous spring. This ability of waterfowl to return to the very location from which they first learned to fly is called homing. It is most dominant in females and stronger in some species than in others.

Molting

One of the characteristics that waterfowl share with only three other groups of water birds (grebes, loons, and coots) is the fact that they undergo a complete feather molt on their wings, which leaves them flightless for a period of time each year. This is a very vulnerable time lasting three to five weeks. Drakes appear very similar to adult females during this pre-fall period. This is of some significance to hunters, particularly those in the northern states and Canada, where distinguishing between some male and female ducks may be nearly impossible under early hunting conditions. The period of total molt is called the eclipse molt or hiding plumage. American Indians referred to this summer phenomenon as "the time when the wild fowl hide their shame."

Another result of this eclipse molt is that adult female ducks typically molt later than drakes. More vulnerable from the late molt, the adult breeding female falls victim to hunter and predator at a greater rate than drakes.

Recruitment

In the fall following a successful nesting season, the young of the year will exceed the numbers of adults. The addition of young waterfowl to the fall flight is called recruitment. Waterfowl managers place great emphasis on this figure, as it is the most meaningful way of measuring the productivity of the habitat and breeding populations.

Because all North American duck species show a population imbalance favoring males, it is readily apparent why hunters should be encouraged to spare females whenever possible. Until now, only the hen mallard has officially been singled out for such protection, but hunters themselves can voluntarily establish a personal code of hunting behavior that could have a profound impact on the future of the sport.

Perhaps the ultimate "trophy" for the advanced waterfowler is not the beautifully plumaged drake in his bag, but rather the solitary, drab female he allowed to alight in his decoys and depart unharmed to breed another year.

Renesting

One of the most common misconceptions among hunters is the idea that waterfowl, like mourning doves, normally hatch and raise more than one group of offspring each nesting season. This false notion is encouraged by official waterfowl management reports mentioning a "second hatch." Waterfowl will make repeated nesting attempts only if their nests are destroyed by a predator, agriculture, or a late spring snow storm. Only southerly nesting wood ducks have ever been recorded actually hatching and raising more than one brood, and that is very rare.

Photo courtesy of Robert L. Davis, Jr.

Wood ducks nest in swamps and beaver ponds. The survival rate of the ducklings is less than 50 percent.

Photo courtesy of U.S. Fish and Wildlife Service

Sporadic nesting success and habitat degradation have contributed to the decline of canvasbacks. Like many species, they have suffered from drought and the increase of nest-robbing raccoons in the prairie pothole region.

Pintail

Mallard

Black Duck

Gadwall

Wigeon

Shoveler

Wood Duck

Cinnamon
Teal

Blue-Winged
Teal

Green-Winged
Teal

Bufflehead

Ruddy

Ringneck

Lesser Scaup

Greater Scaup

Goldeneye

Redhead

Canvasback

Hooded
Merganser

Red-Breasted
Merganser

Common
Merganser

Trumpeter Swan

Whistling Swan

Canada Goose

Greater Snow Goose

White-Fronted Goose

Lesser Canada Goose

Lesser Snow Goose

Emperor Goose

Black Brant

Brant

Cackling Goose

Ross' Goose

COMPARATIVE SIZES OF WATERFOWL

All birds on these pages are drawn to the same scale.

Harlequin

Oldsquaw

Whistling Ducks

Surf Scoter

Common Scoter

White-Winged Scoter

Common Eider

Waterfowl Identification and Behavior

Note: This section contains brief descriptions of waterfowl most commonly encountered by hunters. See the full-color illustrations at the back of this book. For more extensive information, refer to the *NRA Hunter's Guide* or *Ducks, Swans, and Geese of North America,* published by Stackpole Books, Harrisburg, PA 17105.

Geese

The representatives of the true geese that inhabit North America include the following species and subspecies:

- **Canada goose:** Atlantic, Interior, Dusky, Vancouver, Giant, Western, Taverner's, Richardson's, Lesser, Aleutian, Cackling
- **Snow goose:** Lesser, Greater
- **Ross' goose**
- **White-fronted goose:** Lesser White-fronted, Tule goose
- **Emperor goose**
- **Brant:** Atlantic brant, Black brant (Pacific)

Geese have been further divided into 28 continental populations for management purposes. These subpopulations of geese can be identified because they breed together in the same areas, migrate along the same corridor, and utilize the same wintering grounds each year. Waterfowl managers subdivide geese to manage individual populations to their needs.

The greater snow goose has responded to management by recovering from a dangerously low population level of only a few thousand birds at the turn of the century to a very healthy, huntable population of more than 200,000 today.

The Ross' goose, managed separately from its similar-appearing and much more abundant counterpart, the lesser snow goose, appears to be increasing its numbers and expanding its range.

The Pacific populations of lesser white-fronted geese and tule geese have decreased in recent years and are being managed more intensively than the interior white-fronted geese, which appear to be thriving.

Brant populations are most closely tied to weather and vulnerable aquatic food resources. The resulting fluctuations in their numbers can be drastic, but specific management has stabilized them.

Photo courtesy of R. L. Davis, Jr.

While recent fall flights of ducks have been dismal, most species of geese have increased or held their own overall in the last decade, the result of good management and high nesting success.

CANADA GOOSE.

Among the most easily identified of all waterfowl, the Canada's resonating honk, drab-colored body with black and white head, and V flock formation are familiar to most people. With the phenomenal population growth since the 1940s, Canada geese are becoming a more frequent sight across its broad North American range.

A general rule is that as the races of Canada goose get larger, their voices are lower, their wing beats are slower, their flock size is smaller, and their calling is longer on the low note, and less frequent.

15

The small races of Canada goose nest in the arctic and winter along the Gulf Coast, whereas medium and large races of Canada geese are subarctic nesters that winter as far north as weather allows. The unusually warm winter of 1986-87 saw a flock of Canadas numbering 150,000 spend the entire winter in southwestern Minnesota!

The giant Canada goose in recent years has developed a liking for urban environments. Canadas prefer grazing on grasses; mowed lawns and city lakes are raising so many geese that they have become a nuisance in cities in Minnesota, Michigan, and elsewhere.

The main reasons for the tremendous increase in Canada geese is their ready response to refuges on their key migration routes, combined with carefully managed harvest rates and their ability to thrive on agricultural products. In addition, giant Canadas have a naturally high nesting success and brood survival rate.

LESSER SNOW GOOSE. Until 1961, the lesser snow goose and the blue goose were believed to be separate races. Today we recognize them as color phases of the same race. The lesser snow goose, weighing an average of 5 3/4 pounds, is slightly lighter in weight and smaller than the white-fronted goose.

The adult snow goose, as the name suggests, is almost pure white with black wing tips. An occasional individual has a rust-colored head, the result of feeding in iron-rich soils. They have rosy red feet and legs, and pink bills.

Immature lesser snow geese are generally a dirty gray on the top side in flight, while the underside appears nearly as white as the adults. The young also have the characteristic black wing tips similar to adult snow geese.

The blue phase of the lesser snow goose is the same as the white phase, but with a much darker body.

Lesser snow geese tend to fly in large flocks and are the most vocal of all North American waterfowl. Their high-pitched "barking" can be heard for a mile or more.

Spring migration finds in excess of 1 million lesser snow geese advancing northward through Missouri, Iowa, South Dakota, and North Dakota, eating their fill of waste grain all along the way.

Lesser snow geese have been observed wintering farther north in recent years, although not to the extent that the larger Canada geese do. The majority still winter along or near the Gulf Coast in Texas or

The snow goose has become so prolific in recent years that game managers have set liberal bag limits and long seasons. Even so, consistently taking Snow geese is no easy task.

Louisiana, or in central California, with a few wintering in Mexico. Cultivated rice has become an important winter food.

Lesser snow geese show a strong tendency to nest for the first time in their third year, making them one of the latest species of all waterfowl to mature.

GREATER SNOW GOOSE. The greater snow goose is nothing more than a slightly larger subspecies of the lesser snow goose. It averages a pound heavier at about 6.75 pounds and is slightly larger.

Since the breeding and wintering ranges of the two species sparingly overlap, the opportunity for comparison is nil. There is no dark or blue phase in the greater snow goose.

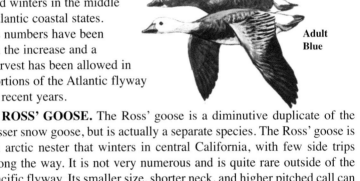

Immature

Adult

Immature Blue

Adult Blue

The greater snow goose breeds in the high arctic and winters in the middle Atlantic coastal states. Its numbers have been on the increase and a harvest has been allowed in portions of the Atlantic flyway in recent years.

ROSS' GOOSE. The Ross' goose is a diminutive duplicate of the lesser snow goose, but is actually a separate species. The Ross' goose is an arctic nester that winters in central California, with few side trips along the way. It is not very numerous and is quite rare outside of the Pacific flyway. Its smaller size, shorter neck, and higher pitched call can help hunters distinguish it from the lesser snow goose.

WHITE-FRONTED GOOSE.
The white-fronted goose is a medium-sized goose averaging six pounds that rarely strays from the Central and Pacific flyways. White-fronts appear uniformly dark at a distance with no obvious distinguishing characteristics. With the aid of binoculars, one should be able to spot the white face patch located just behind the pinkish bill of the adult birds. Specklebellies, as hunters are fond of calling them, derive that nickname from

Immature

Adult

the dark brown to black bars and blotches appearing on the bellies of the adults. Juvenile white-fronted geese are almost impossible to distinguish from immature lesser snow geese in the blue phase when viewed from a distance. Up close, the immature white-fronted goose reveals a yellowish bill and legs, whereas the immature lesser snow goose has a grayish bill and legs. The most reliable clue is their unique, high-pitched, laughing call. Traveling in large flocks, white-fronted geese are almost as vocal as the lesser snow goose.

White-fronted geese breed in the arctic and winter in the mild climates of the Gulf Coast and central California along with most of the lesser snow geese. A few winter in Mexico.

In migration, white-fronted geese take advantage of a variety of crops, but their preference is commercial rice.

Although the white-fronted goose population has shown a steady increase in the Central flyway, the Pacific flyway has shown a steady decline. Not nearly as numerous as Canada and lesser snow geese, the white-fronted goose remains a favorite of hunters because of its fine sporting qualities and its reputation as superior table fare.

ATLANTIC BRANT. This three-pound goose of the Atlantic flyway winters mainly off the New Jersey coast. During the 1930s, the Atlantic brant had to switch from the disappearing eelgrass, its favorite food, to other substitutes. Sea lettuce appears to be the most favored substitute.

The brant is the swiftest goose in flight, more closely resembling ducks than geese. Its short neck, rapid wing beat, and small size belie its goose lineage. In flight the Atlantic brant appears almost black, with the exception of its white belly. Rather drastic population fluctuations in this species have resulted in equally drastic fluctuations in the hunting regulations, but it appears to be holding its own overall.

Black Brant

Atlantic Brant

Waterfowl that nest in the Arctic, like these black brant, endure long migrations and high mortality. Unlike southern-nesting waterfowl, most arctic birds do not renest if their clutches are destroyed. Severe weather and predators can wipe out nearly all nests in a large area.

BLACK BRANT. The black brant is almost entirely a resident of the Pacific flyway, where it traditionally winters in Baja, California for a brief period before heading north in late winter. It is during this period that this little three-pound goose is hunted.

The black brant is considerably darker than its Atlantic Coast counterpart, especially on its belly and breast, where it is a uniform dusky brown. The white neck mark, common to both subspecies, is more noticeable in the black brant than in the Atlantic brant adults.

The eelgrass, so highly prized by brant, has remained abundant on the Pacific Coast. Since both populations of brant nest farther north than other geese, they are especially affected by adverse weather during their critically brief nesting season. Brant have been the least adaptable of all the geese when it comes to converting to agricultural food sources, preferring their traditional (and highly vulnerable) aquatic habitats.

Ducks

Ducks differ from geese, swans, and whistling ducks in several respects. Unlike the true geese, ducks typically molt twice a year, pair off only briefly (usually one breeding season), engage in elaborate courtship displays, and only the female performs incubation and brood rearing.

The subfamily of ducks is divided into four groups:

- **Dabbling (puddle) ducks:** mallard, pintail, gadwall, wigeon, northern shoveler, blue-winged teal, cinnamon teal, green-winged teal, black duck, Mexican duck, Florida duck, mottled duck, wood duck.
- **Diving (bay) ducks:** canvasback, redhead, ring-necked duck, lesser scaup, greater scaup, ruddy.
- **Diving (sea) ducks:** bufflehead, American goldeneye, Barrow's goldeneye, hooded merganser, red-breasted merganser, common merganser, oldsquaw, Harlequin, king eider, spectacled eider, Steller's eider, common eider, black scoter, surf scoter, white-winged scoter.
- **Whistling ducks:** fulvous, black-bellied.

Although the wood duck technically belongs in a separate group known as perching ducks, the similarities in appearance, habitat preference, and habits make it practical to list them among the dabbling ducks.

Dabbling (Puddle) Ducks

The dabbling duck tribe is the most widespread and abundant group of ducks. It is the group of waterfowl most familiar to people and is of greatest importance to sport hunting and viewing. Included in this group are the widely distributed mallard and the secretive wood duck...the "backyard," "down home" ducks that can be seen from the kitchen window and flushed from the creek on the way to school.

They are, as a group, considerably more agile on land than the diving ducks because their legs and feet are positioned farther forward on their bodies, causing them to "waddle" when they walk. The dabbling ducks are also noted for their ability to leap vertically into the air when taking flight and their preferred habit of "dabbling" with their rumps in the air (even though they are capable divers) when feeding in shallow water or on weeds just below the surface. The speculum or colored wing patch is usually an iridescent bright blue or green, as opposed to the typical gray or white speculum found on most diving ducks.

Duck Differences

Diving Duck — Puddle Duck

On Water

Takeoff

On Land

Feet

Flight

Feeding

—DOUG PIFER

The dabbling ducks are usually, but not always, associated with shallow, fresh water marshes, ponds, rivers, streams, backwaters, flooded timber, beaver ponds and lake margins. Their highly adaptable feeding habits also explain their fondness for agricultural fields such as corn, wheat, barley, millet, sunflowers, soybeans, and many others.

Dabblers, especially mallards and wood ducks, frequent woodlands, both flooded and dry, in search of acorns, nuts, and berries.

The overwhelming importance of the dabbling ducks to waterfowlers in the United States is evidenced by the fact that mallards, wood ducks, green-winged teal, and blue-winged teal usually comprise around 75 percent of the U.S. duck harvest and rank 1, 2, 3, and 4 in the bag. Mallards alone usually account for about 35 percent of our duck harvest.

Photo courtesy of R. L. Davis, Jr.

Dabbling ducks usually "tip up" to feed, though they also swim underwater to a lesser extent than the diving ducks.

23

Photo courtesy of R. L. Davis, Jr.

The ability to spring from the water sets dabblers apart from diving ducks, which must pump their wings as they run across the surface to get airborne.

MALLARD. The highly prized mallard is the most abundant and widely distributed duck in North America. Most forms of domestic ducks have their roots in the mallard.

The mallard drake is a large duck with green head, chestnut breast, and white ring around its neck. In flight, the blue-violet wing speculum and white tail feathers can also help distinguish the drake mallard. The broad wings of both drake and hen and a shallow wing motion make it look as if the mallard merely "loafs along," in comparison

Drake

Hen

Drake

Hen

Typical Flock Pattern

Mallards, the most abundant and widespread of any waterfowl in the northern half of the world, are the most important to hunters.

with other ducks. The female is a large, brown duck with whitish underwings and a conspicuously darker breast, sometimes fooling the novice hunter. On a cloudy day, the contrast between the female mallard's dark chest and her light breast and belly can falsely indicate "drake," especially when passing overhead. The experienced hunter learns that, while his eye is attracted to the darker form of the overhead female, he must rely on seeing the *white* tail feathers or neck ring of the drake in order to be certain of his target, lest he shoot the hen by mistake.

A pair of 7 x 35 binoculars is an invaluable aid in assisting the hunter to identify waterfowl *before* they fly into shotgun range. With a little practice, the hunter will not only learn to better identify different species, but will become adept at spotting the drakes in the flock and be better prepared to selectively harvest the drake and spare the hen when the moment of decision arrives.

The female mallard is the most vocal of all the commonly hunted species of ducks. As fall advances, hens seem to become more vocal. This sociable, vocal tendency makes mallards susceptible to good calling imitations by hunters and endears them to call manufacturers. The female mallard often utters a dozen or two lusty, loud quacks in rapid succession. The voice of the drake mallard, like drakes of most other duck species, is much more subdued.

Photo courtesy of M. Embrey

A pair of binoculars can help a waterfowler identify species and sex before the birds get within shooting range.

Although the mallard is the most abundant and widely distributed duck, it is truly a duck of the prairie parkland region of southern Canada. Over 50 percent of North America's mallards typically breed in the southern portions of Manitoba, Saskatchewan, and Alberta. Here the population densities are very much related to the number of ponds available to the ducks each May. The more ponds, the more breeding territories and the more pairs of mallards that can be accommodated.

Always in a hurry to return to the breeding grounds, mallards, along with pintails and Canada geese, are the first waterfowl to head north in the spring and begin nesting.

In the fall it is quite the reverse for the hardy mallards, as they (and black ducks) are the *last* dabbling ducks to head south, and millions of mallards winter as far north as weather and food supplies permit.

As fall progresses, about 10 to 20 million mallards begin filtering down the four flyways, rather equally distributed between the Pacific and Central flyways, but notably more abundant in the Mississippi flyway and relatively sparse in the Atlantic flyway. Funneling in the mid-Mississippi River Valley results in one of the most incredible concentrations of waterfowl in North America, as several million mallards make themselves at home in the flooded timber, soybean, and rice fields of the ancient Mississippi River Delta, between northern Missouri and the Gulf of Mexico.

BLACK DUCK. The black duck, highly prized and formerly abundant on the East Coast, is also found in the Mississippi flyway.

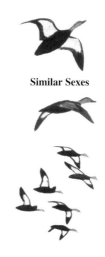

Similar Sexes

The black duck very much resembles the mallard in shape, flight characteristics, and size. It is so similar that it has often been called "black mallard." The two species sometimes interbreed, resulting in hybrid birds that bear some of the traits of each parent. The black duck is much darker than the hen mallard, which both the drake and hen black duck resemble. The dark body of the black duck offers great contrast in flight to the white underwings, and the contrast between the tan head and darker body of the black duck is another distinguishing characteristic that differs from the overall brownish appearance of the hen mallard. The black duck bears an almost purple speculum on its wing with little or no white border, whereas the mallard speculum is lighter blue and has a fairly visible white border along the front and rear edges. Also, the tail feathers of the black duck are dark, not white like the mallard.

Unlike the mallard, the black duck is usually seen in smaller flocks of six to 24 birds. The voices of the male and female black duck are identical to the voices of the drake and hen mallard.

27

While breeding mallards show a strong preference for the prairie parklands, the black duck definitely prefers the more easterly mixed forest areas of the Great Lakes and St. Lawrence Seaway. In their typical habitats along the Atlantic Coast, black ducks are equally at home on salt, brackish, or freshwater marshes, where they exhibit a wide range of food preferences.

Since 1955, black duck populations have declined 60 percent! Because this decline could not be explained by drought, loss of habitat, or overharvest, it has baffled waterfowl managers for years. It was believed that hybridization and interspecies competition with the mallard were likely causes of this steady decline. Studies now suggest air pollution has increased the acidity of breeding habitat and caused the dramatic decline in black duck numbers.

This increase in the acidity of lakes and ponds is caused by acid rain, which destroys food organisms that are critical to waterfowl reproduction and brood survival. The possible effects of acid rain on early nesting waterfowl such as black duck are even more alarming when one considers acid shock. This is what happens when rapid spring runoff dumps an entire winter's accumulation of acid-laden snow into sensitive breeding areas.

Black ducks are among the earliest spring migrants. They are also early nesters, preferring to nest on dry land near water and in fairly dense cover.

Prior to southward migration in the fall, many black ducks actually fly north and west to Hudson Bay and the Canadian prairies. Although they begin arriving in New England early in the fall, they linger in these fairly northern climates until ice forces them southward.

An estimated 3¾ million black ducks made up the fall migration during the 1950s. Two-thirds used the Atlantic flyway and one-third used the Mississippi flyway. By the mid 1980s only 1½ million black ducks were to be found heading south in the fall.

PINTAIL. The pintail or "sprig," one of the more abundant ducks, has been called "the greyhound of the air" because of its trim appearance and swift flight. These ducks are slender with long, narrow wings and tails. Pintails on the water are elegant and float higher than most dabblers. The drake pintail, in breeding plumage, has a chocolate-brown head with the white foreneck extending upward as a stripe onto the back of the head.

The upper body feathers of the female pintail are dark brown and the head and lower body feathers are buff or gray and spotted with tan, giving the bird a streaked appearance. The tail of the hen' pintail is not as pronounced as the drake's.

Drake

Hen

Pintails are most common in the West, but are found in all four flyways. They frequent small waters and often feed in grain fields.

Flight of the pintail is characterized by erratic flying at higher altitudes before leveling off to land. Drakes have a whistling call, while hens make a coarse quack.

Drake

Hen

Typical Flock Pattern

WOOD DUCK. Wood ducks or, "woodies," inhabit creeks, rivers, flood plains, lakes, swamps, and beaver ponds. Over much of the year, wood ducks occur in pairs or in flocks of four to 15, but hundreds may gather at fall and winter roost sites. The crested heads, broad wings, large rectangular tails, and peculiar calls make the wood duck easy to distinguish.

Drake

Hen

Wood ducks usually flock in small, straight-flying groups. Their wings make a swishing sound audible at closer ranges. Hen wood ducks make a squeal call when alarmed. They bob their heads up and down in flight like no other duck.

Drake

Hen

Typical Flock Pattern

The wood duck drake's beautifully crested head has many hues of purple and green, with two white, parallel lines from the base of the bill and from the back of the eye to the rear of the crest. The hen is more attractively colored than most other dabbling ducks. White rings surround the eyes and trail behind on the sooty-gray, slightly crested head.

The wood duck is often classified not as a puddle duck, but as a perching duck.

BLUE-WINGED TEAL. The distinguishing feature of the blue-winged teal is the large, gray-blue patch on its wing. When the drake is in full plumage, the white facial crescent contrasting with the blue head and neck is unique. The blue shoulder patches are covered by brown feathers when the wings are folded. Bluewing hens are smaller than all other dabbling ducks except for the green-winged teal. They have brown plumage and the gray/blue shoulder patches are their only distinguishing feature.

Drake

Hen

Drake

Hen

In areas south of breeding grounds, bluewings court more actively in the spring than other ducks. Blue-winged teal are poor homers, but great pioneers. They winter primarily south of the U.S.

Bluewings have a reputation as fast fliers, exaggerated because their twisting flight and small size make them appear faster than they are. Flying flocks are usually small and compact. Bluewings make high-pitched peeps and quacks.

GREEN-WINGED TEAL. The drake green-winged teal displays a highly visible horizontal white line between the gray flanks and back, and a cream line extends in a half-circle from the bill above the green eye swatch to the back of the head. It is the smallest of the ducks.

Drake

Hen

Drake

Hen

Most of these birds breed as yearlings, as shown by the large proportion of young birds in the fall population. Green-winged teal migrate in larger flocks than do most other ducks. Sometimes as many as several hundred teal may band together. Although they sometimes migrate during the day, most of their flights are at night.

The green-winged teal has prospered when many other species have not, because they breed north of the agricultural lands of Canada. They winter in the far-southern U.S., Mexico, and Central America.

Typical
Flock Pattern

CINNAMON TEAL. Just over a quarter-million cinnamon teal breed in the western states and British Columbia, comprising a small but important population for water-fowlers in that region.

Drake

Hen

Drake

Hen

Cinnamons are often confused with blue-winged teal during hunting seasons. Drakes appear only slightly redder than bluewing males, and hens of the two species are nearly identical. They have the same blue wing patch and conformation. Distinguishing features are its size (about three-fourths that of the bluewing) and the red eye of the cinnamon drake.

Typical
Flock Pattern

31

Cinnamon teal frequent mountain marshes from the Sierra Nevadas through the Rockies, flying low, fast, and erratically in small flocks.

GADWALL. Found mainly in the central U.S., the drab-colored gadwall bears a strong resemblance to the hen mallard. Drakes and hens, similar in appearance, also have calls often mistaken for mallards. Distinguishing features are the gadwall's whitish speculum and smaller, compact flocks.

Drake

Hen

The gadwall population is small, though their numbers have risen dramatically in recent years.

Drake

Hen

Typical Flock Pattern

WIGEON. Wigeons fly fast with deep wing beats and in tight flocks; their flight is more erratic than that of all other puddle ducks except teals. The main feature of the wigeon is the white rectangular shoulder patch of the drake. In both sexes, the white belly is sharply outlined by the brown chest and sides. When the drake is at rest, the white crown provides a distinctive mark and gives the bird its common name: baldpate. The gray head of the adult hen and

Drake

Hen

Drake

Hen

Typical Flock Pattern

immatures contrasts with the brownish chest and sides. At close range, the bluish, black-tipped bill is apparent in all wigeons, regardless of plumage.

A spooky duck, the wigeon often rafts up in open water until very late in the day, then flies into marshes and ponds to feed. Drakes have a whistle call, while hens make a low-pitched quack.

SHOVELER. The most impressive characteristic of the shoveler is its extraordinarily long, wide "spoonbill." The bill is not much larger than the head, but its breadth and spoon-shaped tip make it a unique size among waterfowl. Shovelers usually occur in small flocks of five to 10. In flight they are humpbacked and blocky, totally unlike other dabbling ducks. In full plumage, the drake shoveler is very colorful. A green head and neck are separated from a chestnut belly and sides by a white chest. White stripes extend from the upper white breast along the gray-brown back. Many inexperienced waterfowlers have mistaken shovelers in flight as mallards.

Drake

Hen

Drake

Hen

The shoveler's diet of crustaceans and other animal matter has given the bird a reputation as poor table fare.

Shovelers return to the larger sloughs on their breeding grounds in small flocks that break up as paired birds disperse over the nearby ponds.

Typical Flock Pattern

Diving Ducks

The diving ducks are less familiar to people because they do not frequent places of human habitation as do puddle ducks and some geese. Divers generally prefer the big waters of the oceans, bays, and large lakes and rivers. The deep and remote water affords safety.

Some divers can remain submerged for several minutes and swim to great depths. In 1968, oldsquaws were found caught in Great Lakes fishing nets that had been set 240 feet deep. Some divers prefer to swim underwater to safety rather than fly or paddle from danger.

Physically, divers are different from puddlers in that they are generally more drab looking, because they don't have the puddle duck's brightly colored speculum. They have shorter tails, and often use their large feet as rudders in flight. Their feet are often visible behind a flying diver's body. The diver's legs, set back on the body, make for awkward walking. The diver's wings are smaller in proportion to body size, which provides hunters with a quick reference as to whether they are looking at divers or puddle ducks: Divers have shorter, faster wing beats.

Because most divers feed extensively on fish, shellfish, and other animal matter, they have a reputation for being unpalatable. Exceptions are canvasbacks, redheads, and scaup that feed on high-quality submergent vegetation—these are often considered the tastiest ducks.

Diving ducks are classified as bay ducks or sea ducks, designations that do not accurately describe their habitat preference. The main difference between the two types is that bay ducks breed their first year and sea ducks do not breed until their second.

CANVASBACK. Canvasbacks are the fastest flying of the large ducks, but no faster than the smaller buffleheads and teals. "Cans" are about the same size as mallards. Their long, sloping forehead and bill are unique among waterfowl. The white and black belly and inner white half of the wings of males combine in flight to form the greatest expanse of white exhibited by any duck. The female canvasback has a buffy brown head and neck shading into a darker brown chest.

Drake

Hen

Drake

Hen

Canvasbacks nest from the prairie parkland region to the arctic among diverse habitats; near large marshes, ponds, sloughs, and potholes. Canvasback pairs occupy the larger and deeper permanent ponds for feeding, resting, and courting, but use shallower ponds for nesting.

Typical Flock Pattern

They winter and migrate throughout the U.S. and Canada, with the biggest wintering flocks on the mid-Atlantic Coast. Several factors have caused a severe reduction in numbers in recent years, and hunting regulations have been strict.

Canvasbacks have a rapid, noisy wing beat. Drakes make a peep or growl sound, while hens quack. They are among the easiest waterfowl to decoy.

REDHEAD. The redheads are usually seen singly or in pairs and in flocks of five to 15, which are smaller than those of the canvasbacks. At a distance on the water, the male redhead presents dark fore-quarters, a gray back, and black rear-quarters. The gray back is much darker than the canvasback's. The red color of the head is not always discernible, but always appears a lighter hue than the black chest. Female redheads are a tawny-brown; while on the water, no other color can be seen.

Drake

Hen

Drake

Hen

Redheads are often found in the company of canvasbacks; inexperienced waterfowlers find it difficult to tell the two species apart. Redheads are distinguished from canvasbacks by their smaller size and rounder heads. They appear to fly fast in V

Typical Flock Pattern

formation at high altitudes, in irregular flocks closer to the water.

Redheads nest in the emergent vegetation of large marshes and the larger, deeper potholes of the prairies and parklands. The majority of nest sites are over water in dense areas, but are sometimes on islands or dry land.

SCAUP. Scaup or bluebills are most often found on the large bays, sounds, and inlets on the Atlantic and Pacific Coasts. On the water, the greater and lesser scaups appear identical: The males have black heads, necks, and chests separated by gray backs from the black wings and tails. The females are brown, with single white, oval patches around the bills.

In flight, the lesser scaup appears to have white bands only half the length of its wings. The light band runs the entire length of the greater scaup's wing. Both species migrate late, sometimes just before freeze-up.

Greater scaup breed almost entirely in the arctic and subarctic. In open boreal forest, nesting by greater scaup is largely restricted to islands in large lakes. Almost all of the scaup throughout the open and closed boreal forest are lessers. Probably three-fourths of the greater scaup in North America breed in Alaska, the population estimated at 550,000. Greater scaup nest solely on the marshy lowland tundra.

Drake
Lesser
Hen

Drake
Greater
Hen

Drake
Lesser
Hen

Typical Flock Pattern

GOLDENEYE. The common goldeneye is very difficult to distinguish from the Barrow's goldeneye in flight. At a distance on the water, the shape of the adult drake's head is the best distinguishing feature. The crown of the Barrow's is long, low, and evenly rounded, with an abrupt rise in the forehead, and the white mark in front of the eye is crescent-shaped. Under favorable light conditions, the black heads show a purplish gloss in the Barrow's and a greenish gloss in the common goldeneye.

Drake

Hen

Often called whistlers, goldeneyes get this name from the whistling sound they make in flight.

Drake

Goldeneyes move south late in the season, wintering mainly along the coasts and Great Lakes. Common goldeneyes wintering inland prefer relatively fast waters.

Hen

Typical Flock Pattern

BUFFLEHEAD. The bufflehead is a miniature copy of the goldeneye and one of the smallest of all ducks. It can be distinguished from the goldeneye by its size and white markings on the head. It has a rather long tail compared with other diving ducks.

Drake

Hen

Buffleheads breed throughout Canada and Alaska, migrating in mid-fall. They winter throughout the U.S. and Mexico, concentrating along the coasts.

Population studies show that buffleheads are increasing in the Northeast but declining in the far West.

37

Buffleheads can fly straight up in takeoff, unlike most other divers. Their flocks are small and they seldom make calls.

Drake

Hen

Typical Flock Pattern

MERGANSER. The three mergansers—common, hooded, and redbreasted—are characterized by their long tail and long, narrow, serrated bill used to catch fish. This eating behavior has earned the merganser the name "fish duck" and a bad reputation as table fare.

Drake

Hen

Drake

Drake mergansers can be distinguished by their head features—the common has a smooth head, the hooded has a neat crest with a large white spot, and the red-breasted has a ragged crest. All mergansers have long necks held straight out in flight.

The common winters throughout the U.S.; the red-breasted and hooded are mainly coastal birds. Mergansers fly low and fast, with their flocks in straight lines, and they seldom call in the fall.

Hen

(Common)

Typical Flock Pattern

RINGNECK. Similar in appearance to scaup, ringnecks have blue underwings and brownish-black heads, with a white ring on the bill. Their dark backs are the most visible difference from scaup. Contrary to their name, they have no visible ring at the neck.

Over 90 percent of all ringnecks winter on the eastern half of the continent. They frequent smaller water with more cover than most divers.

Ringnecks fly in open formation and seldom call in the fall.

Drake

Hen

Drake

Hen

Typical Flock Pattern

RUDDY. The ruddy duck has an unmistakable appearance with its blue bill and small, stocky body weighing about one pound. It is the only North American duck that habitually cocks its tail upright. Because of this and other characteristics, biologists place the ruddy duck in a class by itself.

Flying in compact flocks, the ruddy duck flies low, fast, and with a rapid wing beat. When surprised on water it often prefers to swim away or dive rather than fly.

The duck nests in the prairie pothole region and the biggest flocks winter on the Atlantic flyway, with smaller populations on the Pacific Coast and lower Mississippi Valley.

Drake

Hen

Drake

Hen

Typical Flock Pattern

OTHER SEA DUCKS. Among the true sea ducks that winter on the open coastal waters and Great Lakes are the white-wing, surf, and black scoters; the eiders, oldsquaw, and Harlequin ducks.

These ducks are characterized by their habits of staying mostly on large coastal waters and feeding on crustaceans and other animal matter. They are generally considered underhunted and easy to decoy, and have a reputation for poor taste due to their diet. However, special treatment by an innovative chef can make them good table fare.

The scoters and eiders are drab, large ducks, while the oldsquaw and Harlequin are smaller and more striking in appearance.

Black Scoter

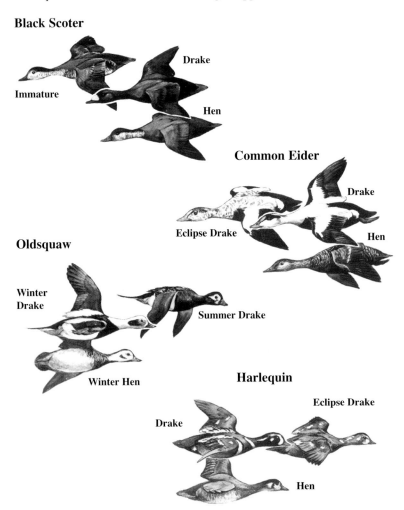

Drake

Immature

Hen

Common Eider

Drake

Eclipse Drake

Hen

Oldsquaw

Winter Drake

Summer Drake

Winter Hen

Harlequin

Eclipse Drake

Drake

Hen

CHAPTER 2

GEARING UP FOR DUCKS AND GEESE

W aterfowl hunting is a gear-oriented sport. While you may be able to jump shoot potholes and small creeks with nothing more than a shotgun, shells, and rubber boots, most waterfowlers find they need a wide array of equipment. This includes special clothing for protection from wind, cold, rain, and water; chest-high boots and boats, motors, and accessories for access to hunting sites; calls, decoys, and portable blinds to fool the game.

Gearing up for ducks and geese can be rather expensive, so most hunters start with the basics, their collection growing with their enthusiasm for the sport.

Photo courtesy of R. L. Davis, Jr.

Waterfowl gear represents a considerable investment, and its quality can mean the difference between success and failure. Inexperienced hunters should seek expert advice before buying.

41

They gradually build an investment that lasts for years and pays dividends in hunting enjoyment. Aside from shotguns and shells, which will be covered later, here's a list of the tools of the trade and what to look for in quality and special purpose.

Clothes

The right clothes can play a part in a waterfowler's success, but most importantly they can make all the difference as to whether he enjoys himself or is miserable.

Boots

Footwear often tops the list, since the waterfowl hunter spends so much time walking where it's wet. A good pair of hip boots or waders is vital. Hip boots are cheaper and make for easier walking and removal. But waders will take you places where hip boots would be submerged—into water about eight inches deeper than hip boots can go—which can be the difference between getting to or not getting to a select hunting area. Waders are also warmer and allow you to sit on wet things without soaking your behind. Sold in a variety of sizes and lengths, waders should have the correct inseam for ease in walking and sitting.

Hip boots and waders are made of either fabric-backed rubber, rubberized nylon, or synthetic rubber. Nylon facing on some models gives a degree of protection against punctures and tears and allows a camouflage pattern to be applied to the boots. It makes boots more expensive but more practical.

Waterproof nylon is the lightest material; if you do much walking and jump shooting, every ounce counts in a heavy pair of waders. Nylon is more difficult to patch than rubber, however. Neoprene waders—with thick synthetic material similar to the fabric of scuba diving suits—are the most expensive at over $200, but are also very warm and buoyant. They are also elastic and closer fitting, allowing more freedom of movement.

Both hip boots and waders are available in insulated models. The best ones have high-topped felt inserts or wool liners. You can get the same degree of warmth by buying a size-larger boot and wearing long underwear and wool socks.

Waterproof boots are notorious for lasting only a couple of seasons, but this is seldom due to their wearing out. Those small holes and tears are easy to fix with a vulcanizing inner tube repair kit or epoxy (duct tape works well for temporary repairs). What really renders boots useless is age and neglect that causes rubber to deteriorate and crack over

Photo courtesy of R. L. Davis, Jr.

A good pair of waders is invaluable in most types of waterfowling. A belt traps air, which provides warmth and a small degree of flotation.

large areas, which is usually irreparable. This is caused in part by ozone, created by a chemical reaction when rubber is exposed to sunlight. To delay this as long as possible, start by buying a "fresh" pair of boots. Try to make sure they haven't been on the shelf for years. After each use, dry them thoroughly—not too close to a heat source—and wipe off any gasoline, dirt, and other contaminants. Keep them out of the sun. When storing them for long periods, hang them upside down, unfolded, in a dry, dark place or store in an airtight plastic garbage bag in a cool area.

You'll need accessories for your hip boots or waders. Boot liners and insoles keep your feet warmer and make the boots easier to dry. Hip boots require a belt to hold them up, while waders need suspenders. A long, wide belt around your waders at waist level also helps trap air for warmth and safety, should you fall in deep water.

If you plan more than a one-day trip, you should include a boot-patching kit. Check before you leave to make sure you don't have any tears—a predawn duck marsh is no place to discover your boots leak.

When you won't be walking in the water, regular hunting boots will suffice. Leather boots are fine for early season, and pacs or sorels are best for late-season goose blinds. Remember, these should be water repellent, because fields are always wet on early morning walks to the pit.

Outerwear

The standard brown canvas duck jacket, with maybe a goose down vest underneath, is still popular in the marshes, but this traditional garb is fast giving way to a whole realm of new styles and fabrics to withstand rain, snow, wind, and cold.

Top-quality waterfowler parkas combine a tough, colorfast, and waterproof shell of nylon or nylon blend with compact, but efficient, insulation. One of the most revolutionary clothing materials is Gore-Tex, an outer fabric made with Teflon. Waterproof but breathable, Gore-Tex contains tiny pores too small to let water drops in, but large enough to let sweat vapor be driven off by body heat.

Parkas made with this fabric are fairly expensive, especially when combined with one of the new lightweight, low-bulk insulation materials. With brand names like Thinsulate and Thermolite, the material consists of extremely thin synthetic fibers that trap more air and hold their collective shape better than other insulations.

These and other materials are being combined into a wide variety of parkas. One of the more popular styles is a waterproof, wind proof, full-length jacket with detachable lining and various accessories. This style capitalizes on the layering effect, which traps more air and allows you to add or subtract clothing for just the right degree of insulation. It offers the best foul-weather protection, and in milder temperatures, the lining can be removed and either unit can be worn as a lighter jacket or vest. The better models are reversible, have a detachable hood, large rear game pocket, hand warmer pockets, neck flap, and other features. Waist-length parkas of this type are made for waterfowlers who stand in deep water and would soak the bottom of a fingertip-length coat. Several companies make these parkas; quality varies, and quality and features are generally proportionate to price. Cost ranges from about $120 to $300, with most just under the $200 mark. Most have matching pants for about $75.

If you can't justify that cost, there is plenty of other good outerwear on the market for less. Keep in mind that very inexpensive usually means cheap, and less of a bargain than it appears. Vinyl rainsuits often last less than one hunt. Superior fabrics are waterproofed canvas and rubber or high-quality vinyl sandwiched in protective layers of nylon or denim. These are usually sold in matching sets of coat and pants.

You may prefer to wear a regular hunting coat and have one of the better-quality rainsuits ready for storms. In this case, make sure the rainsuit is big enough to wear over your cold-weather gear.

Photo courtesy of M. Embrey

Photo courtesy of R. L. Davis, Jr.

When the snow blows, hunters are thankful for modern insulation and shell materials like Thinsulate and Gore-Tex, as well as the new clothing accessories available to waterfowlers.

For extremely cold weather, some waterfowlers wear insulated coveralls or "snowmobile suits." These are the warmest garments; indeed, they can be too warm when the sun comes out or you have to work hard. Wear a lightweight camo shirt underneath so you can layer down, leave the front unzipped, and still be camouflaged.

If you know you'll be completely hidden in a blind, the color and pattern of your outerwear makes little difference. But if you may be exposed—and duck and goose hunters are always more exposed than they think—well-camouflaged clothes are essential. Remember that birds can see color as well as detail. The green pattern you use in the deer woods will not do in a duck marsh. In most cases, camo in shades of brown is best, but plain dead-grass brown may

Photo courtesy of M. Fleming

Convertible waterfowler coats enable the hunter to add or remove layers as the weather changes. They feature both solid-color and camo patterns, warm vests or jackets, and light, waterproof outer parkas.

be suitable for some purposes. When hunting flooded timber, tree bark is a good pattern; it lets you lean up against a tree and blend into the surroundings while allowing full visibility and freedom of movement to shoot. With careful attention to your camouflage, you may not need a blind.

Clothing Accessories

If you've ever frozen your fingers in threadbare gloves or been blinded by the sun because you didn't have a brimmed hat, you know how important clothing details can be.

Hats for the waterfowler must perform several functions. They should be warm, water repellent, camouflaged, and provide shade for your eyes. The epitome of the duck hunting hat is the modified jones type, a crushable style with an extra-long brim in back that keeps water from running down your neck. The best ones are waterproof and insulated with ear flaps. Other favorite hat styles are the traditional jones style with the brim that folds up on the back and sides; the old trooper or woodsman cap with wool or pile earflaps that snap across the crown, and the hybrid of these, the front-brimmed cap with fold-up knit ear flaps. For fair weather, the adjustable baseball-style cap, appropriately camouflaged, is fine.

Some parka manufacturers are making hoods with an extra long top that acts as an eyeshade. Hoods are the warmest and most protective of all headgear, preventing substantial loss of body heat by covering your head and neck with a single unit. They may impair hearing, however.

Gloves, too, come in many forms with different functions. In milder weather, light wool or cotton gloves you can wear while you shoot are the best choice, as long as you know they won't impair your gun handling. These are also good for jump shooting in colder weather, in which your body movement keeps your hands warm. For hunting out of a blind in colder weather, most hunters choose warmer mittens or bulkier gloves, shucking them when it's time to shoot.

There are specialized shooting gloves and mittens. Some of the lighter gloves have a trigger finger made of soft vinyl or other material that greatly enhances sensitivity. Several companies market mittens with a slit in the palm of one hand, designed so you can stick your fingers through the mitten rather than taking it off to shoot. For hand protection with maximum feel, some hunters use fingerless wool gloves or regular gloves with the trigger finger cut off.

On a long, cold hunt in the marsh, it's a good idea to have more than one pair of gloves. They nearly all get soaked, even the water repellent ones, especially when you're handling ducks or decoys. Some duck hunters wear the shoulder-length rubber gloves like trappers use. They go a long way toward keeping you warm when you're working on the water.

If you foresee a lot of standing in cold water, you'll need warm socks and underwear under your waders or hip boots. Wool or polypropylene is superior to cotton in situations where it might get wet. Neither will soak up water as much or as quickly, and both are warmer than cotton when wet.

Other clothing items you should consider for waterfowl hunting include wader belt and suspenders, scarf, face mask, and extra clothes in case your first outfit gets wet.

Decoys and Accessories

The duty of a decoy is simple: appeal to a waterfowl's sense of companionship and lure the bird into shotgun range. But while their function is simple, decoy types and arrangements represent a complex range of theories. Spreads run the gamut of a halfdozen life-size "dekes" in flooded timber to 500 or more magnum blocks on big water. In goose hunting, some hunters do well with rags and bags, while others use

Photo courtesy of R. L. Davis, Jr.

Camouflage face paint or a headnet is the most overlooked part of a waterfowler's gear. An uncovered face peering skyward may spook many birds.

nothing but stuffers—actual mounted geese—that cost over $50 each. Between these two extremes are a wide variety of decoys, each designed for a certain type of hunting, price range, special function, and convenience.

Decoys fit into these general categories:

Solid and hollow floating decoys, made of wood, cork, polyurethane foam, molded plastic, etc., are the most popular among duck hunters. They usually have a weighted "keel" to keep them floating upright, and are connected by rope or are each tied to its own anchor. The hollow plastic types are lighter, more durable, and usually have more detail. The foam types can dent and gouge, but usually float the best. Some hunters get the most satisfaction out of wood decoys, hunting over "works of art" or plain blocks they made themselves. Like most decoys, floaters are available in standard or extra large sizes, and usually cost between $30 and $70 per dozen.

Shell decoys, usually made of molded plastic, are a favorite of hunters after Canada geese in fields. They may be a full body with feet, or just an open-bottom shell, which allows hunters to stack and carry them in large quantities. Some of the shells have removable heads, others are collapsible, while some can be converted to floating decoys for versatility. Shell decoys also come in life-size and magnum versions, ranging in price from around $35 per dozen for the simplest models, made of thick sheets of polyethylene, to over $150 a dozen for the largest, most life-like molded goose shells.

Inflatable decoys are convenient for duck hunters on small, calm waters. These dekes, which are easy to carry and reasonably priced, have a soft rubber body with a three-inch metal ring built into the bottom. The ring acts as a keel and maintains a round opening in the bottom of the decoys. As they are dropped onto the water, air is trapped inside the limp bodies and they inflate automatically. Rubber decoys are painted to resemble various species, but are not as detailed as most molded decoys.

Silhouette decoys have the qualities of being inexpensive and easy to transport. Made from a single sheet of plywood or plastic, they rely on a good paint job for authenticity. They may be staked singly or built into a fold-up stand to hold three silhouettes—which allows them to float for water hunting. The disadvantage of silhouettes is that birds can see only part of your spread—the decoys facing broadside—and wise late-season honkers can get suspicious when decoys seem to disappear as angles of view change.

The hunter in this photo is using stackable plastic goose shell decoys. Although not as realistic as full body style decoys, stackable shell decoys are economical and convenient to haul into hard to get to areas.

Stuffers, as the name implies, are mounted ducks and geese. Few hunters other than those after Canadas bother with stuffers, since they are so expensive to have made. They also are of little use in the rain, turning black when they get wet. But a good spread of stuffers, carefully spaced and with their bases covered up, is the most realistic rig you can have. Canada goose hunters accustomed to using spreads of 200 or more shells often get better results with only 30 or so stuffers.

"Trash" decoys is a term applicable to the decoys used where very large rigs are needed and the game is not hard to fool. Made of painted milk jugs, plastic bags, rags, diapers, or even newspapers, these objects are usually used to fill out a spread. They are most often used for snow geese and sea ducks, but other hunters use a few to supplement their realistic decoys with a few more "bodies." The best feature, of course, is that they are free or very inexpensive. When used in large quantities, they are usually attached permanently to a camouflaged rope for fast layout and retrieval.

Windsock decoys are becoming more popular with hunters who know the importance of movement to give their spreads realism. Wind socks—painted bags that fill with air attached to a plastic stake and head—assume a surprisingly authentic "goose walk" as they waver back and forth in the wind. In a variable breeze, windsocks turn to constantly face the wind—as geese naturally do. Some manufacturers also

Photo courtesy of M. Fleming

Large, full-body goose decoys, with flocked heads are becoming very popular and are so realistic that they can fool even the wariest birds.

sell a brace that will keep the body upright even if there is no wind. There are variations with "spread wings," designed to be staked about six feet off the ground, simulating a landing bird. Standard size runs $50-60 per dozen and magnum sizes considerably more.

Specialty decoys include novelty and special-purpose dekes of various designs. There is the motorized duck decoy, with a battery-operated propeller, to give your water rig life-like movement on calm days. The tip-up decoy—just a vertical duck tail—simulates puddlers feeding. Kites are sometimes used to depict geese hovering or about to land in a spread, and to attract geese from a distance. The strangest long-distance attention getter is the ultimate shell decoy, the decoy blind. Resembling a standard shell decoy, the decoy blind is large enough to contain a hunter and has a flip-open top for shooting. Some hunters add to their rig a confidence decoy or two. These dekes represent a very wary animal such as a great blue heron, seagull, or swan, and are designed to convince shy birds there is nothing to fear.

The type of decoys you choose will depend on your type of hunting and affordability. A full set of decoys, especially for Canada geese, can be more expensive than all your other gear combined. Most hunters start

Successful hunters utilize any means necessary to get their decoys and gear to out of the way places.

with a dozen or two, borrowing or pooling their decoys with companions, until they have their own complete spread.

You'll also need some accessories for your decoys. These may include anchors (the best are thin lead strips, which may be wrapped with the line around each decoy, making a neat package); anchor line, preferably strong nylon; a mesh decoy bag; touch-up paint; and camo rope, if you want to tie the blocks together.

Calls

The beginning waterfowler is faced with a perplexing array of calls, literally hundreds of different ones to choose from. How do you know which ones to buy?

Keep in mind that waterfowl calling is regionalized; the standard technique in the Mississippi Delta probably won't work as well in Puget Sound or off Long Island. Thus the best way to select a call (and learn

Photo courtesy of R. L. Davis, Jr.

Motorized decoys resemble flying or landing waterfowl. They can be so deadly on ducks that some states have made them illegal.

calling technique) is to talk with local hunting friends, call makers, and sporting goods dealers in your area about their favorite calls. Most hunters take at least two calls along to the marsh or field in case the first one malfunctions or doesn't seem to appeal to the birds.

The basic duck or goose call is made of two pieces of hollow wood, plastic, or hard rubber tube, usually round and turned on a lathe. Plastic calls have an advantage in that they will not swell and change tone when wet. Sound is produced by a reed that vibrates when air is blown through the call. Reed duck calls are categorized as hard or soft, hard meaning a raspy sound that is preferred by many callers, though others believe a very hard call can scare off shy ducks. Reeds are usually plastic or metal. Metal reeds are louder, while double reeds sound raspier. There are also whistles that imitate some puddlers such as pintails, wigeon, and wood ducks; there are others that buzz like some diving ducks. Canada goose calls have reeds that change register, from the low moaning sound to the high-pitched honk with an increase in air flow. Prices range from less than $5 for the cheaper calls, to around $25 for

This battery-operated, propeller-driven decoy can add movement to your decoy spread on a calm day. The attraction and realism it provides can make the difference in drawing ducks.

Decoy anchors should wrap line easily then attach neatly to the decoy, to avoid damaging the decoy.

the higher-priced production models, to over $200 for custom-made calls. Expensive custom calls are handcrafted not only for handsome looks but a finely-tuned sound, as well. More expensive is not necessarily better in this case; technique is more important than the type of call you buy.

Tube calls have a rubber diaphragm stretched over the mouthpiece of the call. They are very effective, but they are more difficult to learn to use.

Along with the traditional mouth-blown call, there is also the hand-operated bellows/hose type. This device is especially useful for hunters who haven't mastered the "feeding chuckle" on a mouth call, but most experts agree it's best to learn to use a mouth call.

Along with your call, you might want to buy records or cassette and video tapes with instructions and examples of how to call. There are some excellent tapes that can be a great asset to learning how to call. You should also have lanyards to hang your calls around your neck.

Most hunters take at least two calls along to the marsh or field in case the first one malfunctions or doesn't seem to appeal to the birds.

Boats

Outside of field hunting and jump shooting, a boat is a basic tool of waterfowling. It takes you where the birds are, helps you set decoys and retrieve downed birds, and serves as a blind.

A boat should give you the best compromise between portability, cost, and ability to handle large loads or large waves. Consider horsepower rating, cargo capacity, and the type of water you plan to hunt before buying a boat. Each style has its own good and bad characteristics.

The standard duck boat of today is the 10- to 20-foot john boat or semi-V hull. Hunters like them because they are stable, and the smaller ones are light and maneuverable with motor, oars, or push-pole. They are also easy to turn into a blind; some boats of these styles are custom made for the duck hunter with an aluminum blind framework and are painted olive drab or a marsh grass camo pattern.

Serious waterfowlers still use a modern design of the old sculling skiffs or layout boats. These shallow-draft, low-profile crafts are excellent for sneaking up on flocks, or with good camouflage they can serve as an open-water blind. The bows of these duck boats are partially covered with a deck forming a smaller cockpit surrounded by a three-inch-high coaming, kayak style, to keep water out.

Canoes and kayaks are fine for waterfowling as long as you don't overtax their stability limitations. They are best suited for small water-float hunting and setting up on potholes. They can provide access into the tangled waterways of beaver ponds, where the most puddlers and fewest hunters are often found.

Some models of kayaks have the feature of folding up for transport or storage, which adds considerably to their convenience. There are also foldable boats in a semi-V design. These folding styles are a bit more expensive than the rigid designs, averaging $750-$1,000.

Rubber rafts are used by a few waterfowlers, especially on big-river float trips or on smaller inland water. The obvious drawback of inflatables is the possibility of having a serious tear, and the dangers of having to abandon ship in the heavy clothes and cold water typical of waterfowl season. The big advantage is that you can have an easily portable boat that will carry a big payload. There are many inexpensive makes on the market, but you'll have to pay more for one that's durable and reliable.

A smaller version of the rubber raft is the belly boat, an increasingly popular item for hunters as well as fishermen. The belly boat is simply one or two inner tubes with a tough, puncture-resistant cover and a harness to suspend you in the middle. Usually used with scuba-style flippers, the belly boat offers the most in portability, maneuverability, and economy; you can go places you could reach no other way with a belly boat. Drawbacks are that you can't carry much more than your gun, shells, and a dozen or so decoys. Also, they make a good boat but a lousy cold-water blind; you can stay well hidden in one, with half your body underwater, but you can get cold quickly in later season.

Boat Accessories

If you do much duck hunting from a boat, you'll eventually find yourself in a situation where a well-running motor is critical. There will also come a time when there is no way to get your motor to start. The trick is to make sure these two situations never occur at the same place and time.

Most waterfowl hunters devote more time and money to motors than to boats. The degree depends on how much you have to depend on your motor. A finicky motor is fine if you could almost as easily row or pole

Photo courtesy of M. Embrey

Photo courtesy of R. L. Davis, Jr.

Canoes, kayaks and other small boats can get waterfowlers into isolated ponds, creeks and marshes that conventional boats can't get to.

your boat to where you want to go. If you don't have that option, make sure your motor is in good running condition.

The average 15-foot duckboat needs no more than a five, or maybe 10, horsepower motor. The extra power of the larger motors is wasted most of the time, when you have to go slow, and their extra weight hampers you when you have to lift, pole, or row. If you're going on big water, however, you may need more horses to race a storm to shore or buck winds and waves.

For smaller jobs, the little two-cycle, air-cooled outboards are often best. Costing under $350 and weighing less than 20 pounds, they are easy on your back and your pocketbook. These motors are usually three horsepower or less.

Even if you have a good motor, you'll need oars, paddles, or push-poles as a back-up means of locomotion. For very shallow, mucky water, the "duck bill" push-pole is best. It is a pole with metal blades on

Photo courtesy of R. L. Davis, Jr.

Commercial camouflage material makes it fast and easy to set up a good blind on boats or shorelines.

Photo courtesy of R. L. Davis, Jr.

Photo courtesy of R. L. Davis, Jr.

Many waterfowlers consider moveable blinds to be an important part of their hunting outfit. Portables range from the traditional boat blinds to new inventions such as the pop-up, one-man field blind.

the end that expand as you push, giving you more surface area to push against so the pole won't sink far into the mud. As you pull the pole back up, the blades close to allow easy extraction. Some models have interchangeable tips that let the pole also serve as a stake, paddle, or hook.

Another necessary item for hunting on water is a life preserver. Because a gunner can't be encumbered by the regular bulky lifejacket, many waterfowl hunters wear a camouflaged flotation coat. This style of coat is both buoyant and warm without interfering with movement. Another choice is the inflatable vest that is activated with carbon dioxide cartridges or can be inflated orally. Some hunters just use buoyant boat cushions, but these are not as safe as flotation devices that are worn at all times.

Other Accessories

Some other accessories you might consider for waterfowling include the following:

- Shotgun sling, with looped ends or snap-off swivels for fast removal.
- Shooting glasses, dark for sunny days and yellow to increase contrast on overcast mornings.
- Gunner's gear bag or five-gallon plastic bucket (camouflaged) to hold shells, various hunting equipment, coffee, and lunch.
- Looped game straps to carry bagged game, if you have no other means.
- Binoculars.
- Portable blind or extra camouflaged material.
- A trained retriever.

CHAPTER 3

RETRIEVERS: THE WATERFOWLER'S BEST FRIEND

You did your pre-hunt scouting and set-up at just the right spot before daylight. Decoys were set, your calling worked, your shooting was true. Now you have ducks down on the water . . . how are you going to pick them up?

This is where your trained retriever earns his keep. You may know the adage, a trained retriever conserves game. How so? Because a good dog will recover game in cover that no one could find without a dog and every lost bird added to the bag is one less removed from the wild.

A trained retriever is steady; he waits quietly by your side until sent to retrieve. He will "mark," or watch and remember the location of

Photo courtesy of Pat Nolan

A good retriever is a joy to take hunting. Properly trained dogs can save work and increase the bag. Undisciplined, however, they have the opposite effect.

downed birds; when sent proceed directly to the area; and find and return to deliver them to hand. He will "handle" on blind retrieves, taking whistle, voice, and hand signals to retrieve birds he did not see fall. Perhaps the greatest asset of the trained retriever is his nose. Once he gets to the area of a downed bird, he will use his keen powers of scenting to recover birds that have fallen or have hidden in cover.

How do you go about finding a good hunting retriever? You can buy a pup and train him yourself, or you can buy a trained dog. If you choose to buy a finished retriever—likely costing in the thousands of dollars—you'll have the chance to evaluate him to see if he can do what you want a hunting dog to do. You cannot do this with an eight-week-old puppy. When you buy a puppy, you are buying a promise with the hope that he fulfills it one day. The odds are your puppy will closely resemble his parents and grandparents in temperament and abilities. Therefore, the best way to pick a pup is to pick the pedigree. Don't buy a pup from unproven breeding stock.

If you choose to go with a pup, first decide which breed best suits you. Then choose a litter from parents that have proven themselves in

Photo courtesy of M. Fleming

A retriever can be a vital element of the hunt or just another added pleasure in waterfowl hunting.

Photo courtesy of Pat Nolan

Discipline in a waterfowl dog begins with discipline in the trainer. It takes a studied knowledge, patience, and many hours of work to produce a finished dog with all the attributes of a trained retriever.

the field or competition and have the necessary health clearances for your breed.

Which Breed Is Right for You?

Often, differences within a breed are greater than between breeds. Use these descriptions as a starting point for further research. If possible, spend time with several dogs of each breed you are considering before you decide which is right for you.

The Labrador Retriever.

The Labrador Retriever dominates in field competitions and duck blinds across the country. A medium-size dog, females average from 55 to 70 pounds and males from 65 to 80 pounds. The Labrador has a short, dense double coat needing no real grooming but offering superb protection from the elements. These retrieving machines are tough in the field but very trainable. The Labrador comes in three colors: black, yellow, and chocolate. Yellow and chocolate lines have suffered in times past from breeding done more for color than working ability. However, recent years have seen a resurgence in hunting and competition Labradors of color.

The Golden Retriever.

Smart, quick learners, the Golden, like the Labrador, has his origin in England. The Golden can be less tolerant of any rough treatment in training than the Lab or Chesapeake. The breed standard calls for Goldens to be friendly, reliable, and trustworthy. Golden females aver-

Photo courtesy of Pat Nolan

A well-trained retriever ignores cold water, obstacles, and everything but his handler's commands on his way to retrieve a duck.

age 55 to 65 pounds, the males from 65 to 75 pounds. The Golden coat is longer than that of the Lab, with feathers on the legs and tail, and comes in a wide range of gold colors from a buff to almost red. While part of the attraction of the breed, the coat requires a bit of grooming after a day in the field to remove burrs and tangles.

The Chesapeake Bay Retriever.

A distant third in numbers, the hardy Chesapeake Bay Retriever is an American breed, originally bred to retrieve in the icy waters of the Chesapeake Bay. Stories are that the breed used to guard the boat and gear of the market gunners that kept and bred them. The Chesapeake coat, combined with a no-nonsense attitude about work, make this breed fit for hunting under very tough conditions. The Chesapeake dominated the first retriever field trials in this country. Often slow to mature, they can be determined about what they will and will not do and unforgiving of perceived unfairness. The standard says males should weigh 65 to 80 pounds; females should weigh 55 to 70 pounds. The Chesapeake should have a wooly undercoat and coarse outer coat. They come in a variety of colors: any shade of brown, sedge, or dead grass is acceptable.

According to the American Kennel Club (AKC), 72 percent of all retrievers registered in 2005 were Labradors, and 24 percent were Golden Retrievers. Chesapeake Bay Retrievers numbered slightly more than 2 percent of all retrievers registered. Flat-Coated Retrievers, Nova Scotia Duck Tolling Retrievers, American Water Spaniels, Curly-Coated Retrievers, and Irish Water Spaniels combined to account for the final 2 percent.

Field-bred dogs from the other retriever breeds can be hard to find. While you will have an easier time finding suitable litters from one of the big three breeds, do not automatically rule out a pup from one of the less popular breeds if that is what you want.

Buy a Pedigree, not a Puppy

You say you don't need "fancy papers" on your dog, a retriever is a retriever—you plan to find a healthy looking litter and pick a pup. Well, cows are cows right? All cows can produce milk but if you are starting a dairy you buy Holstein, not Angus cows. Selective breeding works the same for retrievers as it does for cows. Buy a puppy from parents that have proven they can do what you want your pup to grow to do. Pedigrees will tell you everything from whether a dog is proven in performance events to whether he is clear of health disorders. This information will help you select the breeding that is right for you. So, what do all the initials on the pedigree mean?

By helping to fill bag limits with cripples that would have otherwise escaped, retrievers perform their most important function—waterfowl conservation.

Titles and What They Mean

The "CH" preceding a dog's registered name is a "conformation" title designating a show champion, a dog that has been judged as closely matching the ideal physical picture of the breed. This title does not measure working ability and is no guarantee of field talent, but don't exclude a dog from consideration because of the CH title.

Performance titles fall into two main categories, the competitive field trial titles and the noncompetitive hunt test titles.

The competitive field trial events are:

- The derby, a competition for dogs not yet two years old. In the derby, the dog is judged primarily on marking ability.
- The qualifying stake, an intermediate proving ground where dogs are judged on both marks and blinds.
- The all-age stakes, including the "open," the "amateur," and a few restricted stakes. Field Championship points are won in the all-age events. The trials are run over two or three days and usually consist of marks and blinds on land and water.

FC and AFC are the Field Champion and Amateur Field Champion titles won in competitions sanctioned by the American Kennel Club. Canada's counterpart titles are the CFC and CAFC.

A dog with the initials FC or AFC has proven himself capable in tough competition.

NFC is the National Field Champion title awarded to one dog each year at the National Open. NAFC is the National Amateur Field Champion title.

Three main organizations test and title dogs in non-competitive hunt test programs (see box below). These events vary from organization to organization, but they all offer an entry-level title where dogs are judged solely on marking and an intermediate and advanced title with dogs judged on marks and blinds. In the hunt test programs, each dog competes against a standard of performance and not other dogs to qualify at each level.

Resources: Performance Events

Get more information on competitive performance events on the AKC web site at http://www.akc.org/. The Canadian Kennel Club web site is http://www.ckc.ca/.

Non-competitive hunt test programs are offered by:

- The AKC, offering the Junior Hunter, Senior Hunter, and Master Hunter titles.

- The North American Hunting Retriever Association, offering Beginner, Started, Intermediate, and Senior titles. Read more about them at http://www.nahra.org/.

- The United Kennel Club has its own programs for testing and proving hunting retrievers. Read more about them at http://www.hrc-ukc.com/.

You can read about AKC trials and hunt tests at: http://www.working-retriever.com/home.html.

A dog possessing an advanced hunt test title from any of these organizations has proven that they can mark and handle and has demonstrated a high degree of trainability.

Health Concerns

A dog needs to be physically fit and sound to hunt and work in the field. Hips, elbows, eyes, and hearts are all susceptible to genetic disorders that could shorten or end the working career of your retriever. Recently, veterinary scientists have made great strides in identifying heritable diseases in breeding stock.

Photo courtesy of Victoria Diehl

Labrador retrievers are the overwhelming favorite of waterfowl hunters. With good training, the tough, intelligent, even-tempered dogs account for admirable feats in the waterfowl marshes.

Dogs that have tested free of genetically transmitted disorders receive certificates and registration numbers from testing organizations. Some health clearances to look for on the pedigree include the following:

CERF   Canine Eye Registration Foundation
http://www.vmdb.org/cerf.html

CNM   Centronuclear Myopathy
http://www.labradorcnm.com/

OFA   Orthopedic Foundation for Animals
http://www.offa.org/

The AKC Canine Health Foundation and the OFA jointly sponsor the Canine Health Information Center, CHIC, on the Web at: http://www.caninehealthinfo.org/index.html. Their goal is to collect records of health clearances in one central location.

The Web page of your breed's parent club is a good resource for information (see box). You can find out what health clearances are normal for your breed, get information on breeders in your area, and read more about the breed's history and origins.

Photos courtesy of Pat Nolan

The golden retriever (above) ranks number two behind the Lab in popularity among waterfowlers. While it is not as hardy as other breeds, it is a good pet and upland hunter. The strong, bold Chesapeake Bay retriever (below) is considered the toughest, but hardest-to-train, retriever. Characteristics of individual dogs vary greatly.

Resources: Health Clearances

http://www.thelabradorclub.com/	Labrador Retriever
http://www.grca.org/	Golden Retriever
http://www.amchessieclub.org/	Chesapeake Bay Retriever
http://www.fcrsainc.org/	Flat-Coated Retriever
http://www.nsdtrc-usa.org/	Nova Scotia Duck Tolling Retriever
http://www.ccrca.org/index.htm	Curly-Coated Retriever

Photo courtesy of Pat Nolan

When looking for a puppy with hunting potential, it's best to start with reputable breeders. Pups should be purchased before they are two months old to ensure bonding with their new owner.

Buying and Bringing Your Pup Home

Before You Buy

Make sure you get a written copy of the sale agreement and a copy of all health guarantees. Your breeder will give you an application form for individual registration of your pup.

Your puppy should come with a short acceptance period to allow you time to have your vet examine him. Make sure you do. Sometimes a vet will find a defect in a pup that is not visible or noticeable. This first exam can save you much grief and expense later on.

Before you bring your pup home, you should prepare for his safekeeping. You will need a kennel run or a fenced area. When you cannot be with your pup, confine him. A retriever running at large is trouble waiting to happen. Make sure he always has access to fresh water, shade, and a way to get out of the elements.

Once Home

Your new pup cannot regulate his body heat well when he is very young and should not be left out in very cold weather. Once grown, he can do fine with an outside doghouse. See that it has a windbreak, or door, and that it is just big enough for him rather than too large. If his house is too large, his body heat cannot keep it warm inside.

A crate is helpful when housebreaking your pup. Put him in his crate when you cannot watch him in the house. When you release him from the crate, take him directly out to potty. This habit combined with his natural desire to keep his bedding area clean, will make it easier to housebreak him.

Photo courtesy of Pat Nolan

Some pups show a great deal of promise at an early age.

Crate your pup when transporting him in a vehicle. If you keep a crate in the back of a truck, be sure to tie it down to keep it from flipping. Crates need to be shaded in the summer and covered in the winter to protect your dog from the elements.

Health Care

Veterinarians differ on what shots they recommend when, but find a vet you like and follow their advice. Pups need a series of shots for protection against distemper, hepatitis, leptospirosis, parainfluenza, parvovirus (DHLPP), before they are 4 months old. State laws vary on when to give the first rabies shot, usually after four months, so be sure to follow your vet's advice. After that, your dog will need yearly exams and revaccinations.

Most areas of the country now have reported cases of heartworm. The heartworm parasite is spread from an infected dog or cat to a healthy animal by a mosquito bite. Test your dog annually and keep him on a monthly preventative to ensure he is free of this potentially deadly parasite.

Puppies need puppy food until nine - twelve months, then adult dog food. Your retriever is an athlete. Don't try to get by on the cheapest food you can find. Working retrievers should get at least 10 percent (some experts recommend 20 percent) fat content for energy and 25 percent protein to build and maintain strong muscles and bones. Most of the premium performance blends of dry dog food should do just fine.

Retriever field trials encourage the highest levels of breeding and training for hunting dogs.

Training

Puppy Training

The first few months of your puppy's life are exciting and sometimes trying. Remember, they do grow up eventually. Pups need daily attention, exercise, and socialization. Many areas have local clubs or trainers that offer puppy classes. While most of these will be geared toward companion dogs, your retriever will benefit from the early instruction and good manners he will learn.

For years, trainers believed it best to wait a year before a pup should begin his training. For all intents and purposes, your pup's brain is fully functional by the time he is 21 days old. When you take him from the litter at seven or eight weeks, he is ready to begin bonding with you as a working partner.

Try to introduce your pup to the environment and the work he will do before he is six months old. Short daily sessions of play retrieving, and puppy obedience training will teach your pup to enjoy training and working with you. A gentle introduction to water and familiarization with birds will make your job of training much easier.

Rolled socks, tennis balls, or puppy-sized bumpers are great for starting your pup to retrieve. Offer the opportunity to retrieve but do not force the issue. A few retrieves each session will pique your dog's interest and leave him wanting more.

Let your dog drag a light line when you are with him and when he is retrieving. This way, you can teach him early on that he cannot run away.

Formal Training

When your pup is around six months old he will be ready for formal training. Obedience training on basic commands—heel (walking quietly by your side), sit, come when called, and stay—will establish the foundation of control needed in the field. Force fetch or a trained retrieve are the minimum.

No matter how smart your dog is, he doesn't understand English. You must show him what you want him to do for each command. Reward him when he does what you want and gently correct him for disobedience. He will learn more from patient repetition and short daily sessions than he will from marathon lessons once or twice a week.

While your dog may be over the moon to retrieve, he will profit from learning a trained retrieve. This trained retrieve or force fetch will teach your dog that he must pick up when told, hold without dropping, and deliver your ducks to hand. This is a necessary foundation for advanced training in blind retrieves.

With a good program of basic obedience and force fetch, you are ready to begin to simulate hunting situations for your dog. Practice retrieves in different field and water conditions including working from blinds and through decoys. Be sure to introduce your dog to the sounds of your calling.

To introduce your dog to gunfire, have a helper stand at a distance and shoot a blank gun before throwing a bumper or bird for your dog to retrieve. Repeat every chance you get to have someone throw for you. Your dog will benefit from watching marks thrown in front at a distance and he will quickly associate the gunfire with retrieving. Once he does, it is an easy matter to move the thrower gradually closer until he is shooting right next to your dog.

Training is just the start of his education; once he begins to hunt, your dog will continue to learn from every day spent in the field and every bird retrieved.

If you decide you'd like your dog to know the advanced hand signals, try to attend a local competition or two to see what the dogs and handlers are doing. You may meet others from your area and arrange to help throw marks for each other.

Check out the Professional Retriever Trainers Association web site for listings of pro trainers in your area: http://www.prta.net/

Conclusion

Waterfowl hunting is not just about putting ducks in the pot. Much of the pleasure comes from the time spent in the perfection of the skills needed for a successful hunt. Like carving your own decoys or learning to call, training your own dog with the help of others or in association with a training professional, can add immeasurably to your overall enjoyment.

Many hunt test and field trial participants got their first dog just to pick up their ducks only to be bitten by the retriever bug. They have found that retriever training is an enjoyable way to extend their season year-round through preparation for, or participation in, competition.

While your dog can be a year-round invitation to retrieving opportunities, it is also a year-round commitment. Unlike a gun that you can put in a safe at the end of the season and then dust off before opening day, your retriever needs housing, care, exercise, and attention daily.

If you are ready for that commitment, the returns in companionship, devotion, and satisfaction can be phenomenal.

Photo courtesy of M. Fleming

Part II

Shotgun Shooting
For Waterfowl
Hunters

Photo courtesy of R. L. Davis, Jr.

Photo courtesy of M. Embrey

CHAPTER 4

THE WATERFOWL SHOTGUN

Waterfowling presents a special challenge to the shotgun shooter today. The most varied and fast-paced of any wing-shooting, waterfowling requires versatile, accurate, and well-practiced shotgun-handling skills.

It is essential to select a waterfowl gun appropriate for your type of shooting and your personal style and tastes. Considerations include the shotgun's barrel, choke, action, fit, and price. The type of ammo you use may also affect your choice of shotgun.

Workings of a Shotgun

The modern waterfowl shotgun is about four feet long and designed to be fired from the shoulder. It shoots a load of between 50 and 300 round pellets, as opposed to the single projectile fired by rifles and handguns. The pellets form a pattern of about two to four feet in diameter, which allows the shooter to hit small or moving objects easier than with a single bullet.

There are basically three components to a shotgun: the barrel, stock, and action.

Barrel

The smooth-bored shotgun barrels range in length from 18 to 36 inches, with the most popular lengths for waterfowl being 26, 28, and 30 inches. For many years hunters believed that longer barrels shoot pellets at a higher velocity and in a smaller, denser pattern, but the differences have now been found to be insignificant. Barrel length does make a difference in pointing and shooting, however. Most hunters find that a shorter barrel is quicker to swing on sudden shooting opportunities such as flushing birds, while a longer barrel provides a longer sighting plane and a smoother swing for the longer passing shots often presented by waterfowl.

Parts of a Shotgun (Pump)

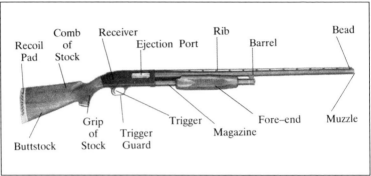

Choke

Most hunting shotguns have a narrowing at the muzzle called a choke. The tightness of the constriction controls the size and density of the pellet pattern. Wider patterns are better for closer shots, whereas tighter patterns enable you to kill birds that are bigger or farther away. The common choke specifications, from the most open to the tightest, include: skeet or cylinder bore, improved cylinder, modified, improved-modified, full, and extra-full. Waterfowlers often use improved cylinder for close decoying ducks, modified for normal duck and goose shooting, and full choke if they expect shots at longer ranges.

The choke works by compressing the pellets together just before they leave the barrel. Generally, the more compressed they are, the tighter the pattern will be. But there are other considerations. Larger pellets tend to make a tighter pattern than smaller pellets for a given choke. In each firing, some lead pellets are deformed through compression or abrasion. Upon meeting air friction, they fly wildly and lag behind the main charge. A pattern with many of these "fliers" has reduced effectiveness.

It's important to test the pellet pattern of your gun and load at various ranges before you go hunting. This is done by shooting large sheets of paper and examining the spread between pellet holes. (Patterning is explained in more detail later.)

Steel shot generally requires a more open choke than lead for a similar pattern. The properties of steel, including its resistance to deformation, cause it to shoot generally tighter patterns than lead shot.

Choke designations are usually stamped on each shotgun barrel, except for those with variable chokes. Most shotgun makers today offer

Photo courtesy of R. L. Davis, Jr.

Screw-in choke tubes add great versatility to a shotgun, "customizing" it for each load and hunting situation. Most shotguns with the feature provide improved cylinder, modified, and full chokes, though skeet and extra-full tubes are also available. Check with your gunmaker before using the choke tubes with steel shot, as larger pellets can damage muzzle inserts.

changeable chokes, either a permanent adjustable knob at the muzzle or the more popular screw-in choke tubes. These options allow the hunter to select the right choke for specific game, range, and load without having to use a different gun. Some hunters believe using the same firearm for all their shotgunning helps them improve their shooting skill; and, of course, it is less expensive than buying additional guns.

Mounted on the shotgun barrel are pointing aids. On many guns this is only a simple bead at the muzzle. Some shotguns have two beads, including one at mid barrel, while others have a flat rib running the length of the barrel used as a sighting plane.

Chamber

Another part of the barrel is the chamber, the near end of the barrel where the shell is held as it is fired. Chambers are designed to hold shells of specific diameters (gauges) and lengths. Shotguns recommended for waterfowl are chambered for 10, 12, 16, and 20-gauge

Shotshells suitable for waterfowl come in an array of sizes, powder charges, and pellet loads, reflecting their wide variety of functions. Common loads range from the heavier 2¾-inch 20-gauge shells through the popular, versatile 12-gauge ammo, up to the massive 3½-inch 10-gauge magnums. The smaller .410-bore and 28-gauge loads have some limited uses for ducks, but only in the hands of expert shotgunners.

shells. Gauges are not interchangeable, though shells of different lengths in the same gauge may sometimes be used. (As an example, many 12-gauge guns have chambers that will accept shells that are either 2¾ or 3 inches long.) Shotguns chambered for a new 3½-inch 12-gauge shell have recently been introduced.

The 10-gauge is the most powerful shotshell, holding the most pellets and powder. The 12-gauge is the most popular waterfowl gun, since it is viewed as the best compromise between economy, versatility, and weight. The standard 20-gauge is not recommended for most waterfowling; a three-inch 20-gauge may be suitable but is too light for large or long-range waterfowl. While ducks have been taken with the smaller 28-gauge and .410 bore, their light pellet charges make them suitable waterfowl guns only for very close-range shooting by expert shotgunners.

Action

Shells are inserted into and removed from the chamber by the shotgun's action. The four types of actions include semi-automatic, pump, hinge, and bolt.

Photo courtesy of R. L. Davis, Jr.

Shotgun actions include, left to right, side-by-side, bolt-action, pump, semi-automatic, over-under, and single shot. Each type of mechanism has advantages and disadvantages over the others. Hunters must choose the style that fits their type of shooting and personal taste.

Photo courtesy of R. L. Davis, Jr.

Pump action shotguns are among the most reliable and continue to be the most popular shotguns for waterfowling.

Semi-Automatic Action

The semi-automatic, or autoloader, is a favorite among waterfowlers, as it allows rapid second and third shots. Another advantage is that the action absorbs some of the recoil of heavy duck and goose loads. The semi-automatic's mechanism is operated by either gasses or recoil from the fired shell, so that each time the shooter pulls the trigger, another round is chambered with no conscious effort. The first shell is chambered manually or by operating a bolt handle and release button. Because of the complexity of the mechanism, the semi-automatic action is the most liable to jam if it is not properly cleaned or is exposed to cold, rain, and ice.

Slide Action

Probably the most popular style is the pump or slide-action shotgun. The pump is reliable and comparatively inexpensive, while being easy and quick to operate. With the pump, the shooter fires a round and then chambers the next by pulling the gun's moveable fore-end toward him. The fore-end rides on a slide as it opens the action, ejects the spent hull, and inserts the next round. When it is returned to the forward position, it automatically locks into place so that it won't slide again until the trigger is pulled or the action is released. Pump shotguns have a button or lever to open or close the action.

Hinge Action

The hinge, or breaking, action comes in three styles, including side-by-side or over/under double-barrel and single shot. To operate a hinge action, a lever on the receiver is moved to one side and the barrel's tip

The pump or slide-action shotgun is operated by pulling the fore-end back to eject the spent hull, then pushing it forward to chamber the next round. The slide cannot be worked again until the trigger is pulled or the action is released.

The hinge action, shown in the over/under design, is tipped open to expose the breech. Other shotgun types with this action are the single barrel and side-by-side. Double barrels give the shooter the option of having two different chokes for different shooting situations.

down, exposing the chambers. (In another design, a lever pulls the breech end of the receiver away from the chambers.) Shells are manually chambered; on some models, spent hulls are automatically ejected when the action is opened. This type of action limits the number of shots a hunter will have, but it also has advantages. Because double-barrels have a recocking trigger or separate triggers, a shooter is not required to cycle the action, and a hunter can generally get two shots off very quickly and accurately. Also, double-barrel shotguns can be obtained with a variety of choke combinations, providing the hunter with a choice of two different chokes. In most cases, such as on decoying ducks, the hunter will fire a more open-choked barrel first at the close-range targets, then shoot a tighter-choked barrel best suited for ducks as they gain distance flying away.

Photo courtesy of R. L. Davis, Jr.

Comparatively slow and cumbersome to operate, bolt-action shotguns are rarely seen in waterfowl hunting today. They are still manufactured in limited quantities, however.

Bolt Action

The bolt-action shotgun was commonly used earlier in the century, but has lost popularity. The bolt-action is quite slow to operate, requiring the shooter to take his hand from the trigger and operate a bolt handle between shots.

Bolt-action shotguns often have a box-style magazine, the mechanism that holds shells ready to be chambered. Most other shotguns have tubular magazines attached underneath the barrel, limited to holding two shells for waterfowl hunting. Shotshells are loaded into the gun by pushing them into the springloaded tube or box magazine at the bottom of the receiver. Some box magazines are detachable.

Safety

Another important part of the action is the safety. Safeties are located in a variety of places—usually under the thumb of the trigger hand or on the trigger guard. It is important to acquaint yourself with the safety and its proper use and location. Safeties can fail; be certain at all times that yours is engaged and functioning properly. Always treat your shotgun as if it could discharge at any moment, regardless of whether the safety is on or if the gun is loaded.

Stock

The stock forms the handle of the shotgun and is held securely by hands, shoulder, face, and neck. Good performance requires that all these "handles" fit with your body proportions. For the most tailored fitting of a shotgun, consult a gunsmith or other expert.

Photo courtesy of M. Fleming

Some hunters choose to paint or tape their guns to remove any shine that may flare wary birds.

An important element of stock fit is the length of the stock, also known as length of pull. To get a general idea of this length on a certain shotgun, first make sure the gun is unloaded and the action is open. Grab the grip in your trigger hand, place your finger comfortably on the trigger, and hold the gun vertically with the stock running along your forearm. If the butt fits in the inside of your elbow with your trigger hand in place, the shotgun has about the right length of pull. If not, the stock should be cut down or lengthened by adding a pad, or you should choose another gun.

The drop at comb is another important consideration. This drop from the plane of the barrels to the plane of the stock determines the position of your head as you shoot. More of a drop allows you to hold your head higher, and vice versa. This is strictly a personal choice; just make sure your selection allows proper shooting form. (More considerations for fit and shooting position are discussed in Shotgun Shooting Techniques.)

Stock styles are generally classified as pistol-grip stocks and straight stocks, which are self descriptive. Straight, or English, stocks usually have a smaller drop in comb than pistol-grip stocks. Waterfowlers usually prefer the surer grip of a pistol-style; straight stocks, which some believe are faster pointing, are used mostly for upland game.

Selecting a Shotgun

The shotgun you select for waterfowl shooting will depend on requirements of the sport and personal tastes. Most waterfowl hunters use a 12-gauge. If versatility is important, remember that certain autoloaders handle many kinds of loads while others are restricted to a certain type of load, and that variable chokes also greatly increase versatility. Prices vary substantially, as does quality. Shotgun characteristics vary also; some shooters dislike the wide sighting plane of a side-by-side, while others are disturbed by the "feel" of certain autoloaders or having to operate the action of a pump.

Consider all the types of hunting you plan to do and all the advantages and disadvantages of different models. If most of your waterfowling is jump shooting, you may want a lighter shotgun that is easier to carry. But many waterfowlers prefer a heavier shotgun than they would use for upland hunting. If you hunt from a blind most of the time, the extra weight is really not a burden and helps reduce felt recoil. An auto loading action will also cut the kick. In a crowded blind, it is not

Photo courtesy of M. Fleming

One way to get a general idea of stock fit is to cradle the shotgun on your forearm, with your finger on the trigger. If the butt fits just inside your bicep, with your arm at a 90-degree angle, the gun's length of pull is about right. Check with a gunsmith or other expert for a more tailored fit.

advisable to use a hinge action, which can be awkward to open and close, or a short-barreled shotgun, which produces a painfully loud muzzle blast. You should consider buying a shotgun with a Parkerized or other non-glare metal finish.

You are well advised to study the different types and makes and perhaps try out different shotguns before buying. A good way to determine if a shotgun has a good natural fit is to close your eyes and shoulder the gun wearing light street clothes. If you open your eyes and find you are looking straight down the barrel, with the thumb of your trigger hand about an inch from your nose, the stock fits your natural pointing style.

Shotgun Cleaning

Keeping your shotgun free from dirt, powder residue, lead buildup, and other contaminants will ensure that it operates as smoothly and lasts as long as possible. You must give special attention to keeping your gun clean if it is subjected to much moisture, salt water, or other corrosive substances, or if it has an automatic action, which can easily malfunction when dirt creates additional friction between moving parts. The excess residue created by steel loads can require more frequent cleaning than conventional lead loads. Ideally, you should clean and oil your shotgun after every day of use. Always make sure to examine and lubricate your shotgun after prolonged storage; frozen or clogged parts could be a safety hazard.

A cleaning kit should contain a variety of tools and products, including cleaning rods and tips, cloth patches, brushes, bore solvent, and oil.

The first step is cleaning the action and receiver, where the most accumulation of harmful residue occurs. This can be removed with a variety of cloths, brushes, and cleaning products. Always wipe solvent from the parts and coat with oil. Pay particular attention to hard-to-reach and moving parts; spray-on oil works best here. It's best to take the action apart for thorough cleaning.

Powder residue also accumulates in the bore. Begin by loosening and removing most of the dirt by scrubbing the bore with a brass brush and/or solvent-soaked patches attached to the cleaning rod. If possible, this should be done with the barrel removed or from the breech end of the barrel. Wipe the bore down and finish with a light coat of oil.

Store your shotgun where it is safe from the effects of moisture. Always make sure your shotgun is dry and oiled before you put it away. It should be stored where dry air circulates in case moisture should condense on the metal or wood parts.

CHAPTER 5

SHOTSHELL LOADS FOR WATERFOWL

W hen it comes to ammo choices available to hunters, no other hunter group has as many as waterfowlers. Steel, tungsten, bismuth, and nickel are just a few shot samples, and there are shotshells available that have combinations of each. Because materials used to manufacture shot are still evolving, the recommendations and discussion in this chapter will be mostly about steel shot, as it is the most popular load among waterfowlers.

Photo courtesy of R. L. Davis, Jr.

When it comes to shotshells, today's waterfowler has many choices. Steel, bismuth, tungsten and nickel are just a few samples of alloys that are available. All have advantages and disadvantages.

89

Waterfowl Load Selection

In the early eighties steel shot was phased into waterfowl hunting and lead shot was outlawed. Essentially, steel shotgun pellets are made of what is called "soft" steel. When tested on the Diamond Pyramid Hardiness scale, it runs about 90 DPH. Ball bearings reach a much harder 270 DPH, while air rifle shot does about 150 DPH. (Do not confuse air rifle shot with steel shotgun pellets. It is considerably harder and can do gun damage). High-antimony lead shot tests no higher than 30 DPH. Thus, steel shot is specialty steel, and it should not be employed in shotguns with thin-walled barrels. Even though it is soft as steel alloys go, it will exert lateral pressures greater than those of lead loads and will harm your barrel. Steel shot should be used in guns with barrels hard enough to handle it. If in doubt, check with a gunsmith or gun manufacturer.

Steel shot selection is nothing like lead shot. For any given shot size (diameter) steel is lighter than lead. A No. 4 steel pellet, for example, does not weigh the same as a No. 4 lead pellet, nor does a steel BB scale the same as a lead BB. This weight differential has a significant three-fold meaning: (1) The steel pellet will loose it's initial velocity and energy values somewhat sooner than lead pellets of the same size and shape, because air resistance slows lighter objects down sooner than it does heavier ones; (2) There will be more steel pellets in any given shot charge weight than there will be lead; (3) Since steel pellets must be larger to match the energy of standard lead loads, you will have fewer pellets in a comparable steel shotshell. Each point deserves some elaboration:

Actual Size	Shot Designation	Diameter	Approx. Number of Shot in 12-Gauge 3" Magnum
●	No. 6	0.11"	366
●	No. 5	0.12"	276
●	No. 4	0.13"	219
●	No. 3	0.14"	180
●	No. 2	0.15"	146
●	No. 1	0.16"	120
●	BB	0.18"	81
●	BBB	0.19"	72
●	T	0.20"	60

Since steel pellets loose their velocity/energy sooner than spherical lead pellets, one must use steel pellets that are two to three sizes larger to approximate the downrange performance of lead shot. For example, steel No. 4s have approximately the energy as lead No. 6s inside 35-40 yards, but thereafter energy falls off quickly. Therefore, steel 4s are certainly not the equivalent of lead 4s. To get a steel shot load that gives the downrange energy of lead 4s, one should choose steel No. 3s, 2s or, better yet, 1s. Steel No. 1 is a very positive duck load despite being considered too coarse for close range on small ducks. By going two sizes heavier than they would normally pick in lead shot loads, hunters will generally find their results improving with steel shot. Some experienced steel users, however, have indicated a need for more effective small-shot loads for smaller, close range ducks.

The same rule applies to goose loads, where it is best to use steel loads three sizes larger than lead sizes. A goose hunter would do well to pick steel triple-Bs (BBB), or T-size pellets for best penetration. There is concern that large steel sizes such as Fs or Buckshot could do barrel damage or be a safety hazard if they reach unseen people. Make sure to check state regulations regarding shot size to avoid safety hazards.

What are good general shot size choices for various types of waterfowling? Some experts believe steel No. 6s should never be used for waterfowl, while some report good results on small ducks at close range. Although steel 6s may fill out a pattern, they are very light and shed velocity and energy quickly. Steel 3s and 4s are the smallest and lightest pellets that can be considered for duck hunting, and they should be applied with restraint. As mentioned before, steel 4s have about the energy of lead 6s, the 3s have a mite more (depending on muzzle velocity of course). Neither size should be thought of as long-range pellets. Both steel 3s and 4s are best kept inside 35 yards for optimum effectiveness, and should never be used for geese. Steel 2s can be successfully used to 40 yards, but are borderline on geese. Three-inch magnum loads will stretch these ranges by 10 percent. Steel 1s are effective on ducks to 40-45 yards, within which range they can also handle geese. Fringe hits with steel 1s will not anchor game, although they tend to do a better job than lighter 2s, 3s, and 4s, because they pack more energy per pellet.

Steel BBs are generally recommended for basic goose hunting. In a tight patterning gun/load they do well on high mallards, too. For improved effectiveness on geese, though, BBBs and T-shot are recommended. While many hunters will opt for the heavier T-shot, BBBs will give some good performances.

The goose hunter's need for extra-large pellets has sparked the re-birth of interest in the 10-gauge shotgun, because its cavernous 3.5 inch hull can hold considerably more BBBs, Ts, and Fs than the 3-inch 12-gauge. Too, the 10-gauge Magnum's bore ratio can generate high ve-locities to enhance the longer-range penetration of these bigger steel pellets. While the "Big 10" packs more power than a 12-gauge, it should not be considered a range extender, and hunters should keep in mind that it takes special skill to master the heavier, bulkier gun.

Patterns and Shot Strings

Shooting ability is a big factor with steel shot because it demands greater perfection than lead loads. Steel stays round and flies more uni-formly, while deformed lead spreads out or strings out in tails, provid-ing a third dimension that makes hitting easier. A hunter could lay the lead load out ahead of the target and though the main mass of the pat-tern may miss ahead of the bird, there is still a chance for the bird to fly into the tailing deformed lead pellets. With steel shot, however, it's a different situation. Because steel shot doesn't deform, its aerodynamics are more uniform; consequently, charges have considerably shorter shot strings and more compact patterns, which give noticeably less leeway for shooter error. When tested on target sheets towed at waterfowl speeds and distances, steel loads impact in nearly the same concentrated mass as they do on stationary patterning sheets. Thus, steel shot requires precise placement because the pattern is small with very short shot strings. Hunters must improve their shooting skills to score consistently with steel. Make a good smooth swing with steel, and it will connect.

When it comes to choke, steel shot's hardness also requires some changes. Whereas hunters who used lead shot boasted about their long-barreled, full choke guns and rifle-tight patterns, more open degrees of choke tend to do better with steel loads larger than 1s. It is quite possi-ble that steel 2s, 3s, 4s, and 6s will pattern well from a full-choked gun, because the shot is smaller and tends to flow easier through the choke constriction. When it comes to 1s, however, the pellets get bigger and do not flow as fluidly through a tightly-choked barrel. Running big steel pellets through such a full choke can result in: (1) ring bulging of the barrel at the start of the choke taper and (2) poor patterns as the pellets bridge together, jam through the muzzle, and jostle each other at exit. In some guns, 1s may move fluidly for excellent patterns and in others they won't. It's a marginal thing, subject to test with each individual gun/load combination. Be particularly careful if your gun has screw-in type choke inserts, as they can be severely damaged by large steel pel-lets.

When it comes to steel shot larger than 1s, less choke constriction appears to work best. The coarse, unyielding pellets simply flow more fluidly through a wider opening. However, some choke constriction is still needed to stabilize and control the charge. In the 12-gauge, for instance, improved and modified chokes handle steel BBs, BBBs and the various buckshot sizes variously better than full choke. Its even been said that the full choke waterfowl gun may be on its way to becoming a memory.

Patterning Your Shotgun and Loads

Different shotgun loads, even two brands with identical specifications, can give amazingly different performances. The only way to truly understand how your shotgun shoots certain loads is to test the patterns at a variety of different yardages. Test firing at paper targets shows whether your gun is shooting where you point, and whether it shoots a good pellet formation. It helps you find the best combination of gun and load, determine your range, and build confidence in your shooting.

Photo courtesy of M. Embrey

Hunters shooting at decoying geese at close range can shoot steel shot sizes as small as No. 1 and No. 2s. Longer ranges and pass shooters should use T and F size.

Use a pattern sheet for the most scientific information on pattern accuracy and density. Draw a bullseye in the center of a large piece of paper, at least 40 inches square. Hang or tack the paper vertically in a safe shooting area. Assuming a steady position, such as sitting or on a bench rest, hold the shotgun's bead at the bottom of the bullseye and fire. Take the pattern sheet down, determine the center of the density pattern, and mark it. Compare this mark to the bullseye to determine the accuracy of the shot; the pattern shouldn't be more than three or four inches off center. Draw a 30-inch circle around the center mark, using a template or large compass. (Make the compass by driving a nail into one end of a wood strip, then drilling a quarter inch hole 15 inches from the nail. Tack the nail into the center of the pattern, hold a pencil into the drilled hole, and draw a circle by pivoting the wood strip around the nail.)

To find the percentage of pellets that struck within the circle, count your hits within the circle, multiply this total by 100, and divide that figure by the average number of pellets in each load. (Yes, you have to cut open some shells and count the shot.) For example, an average 1.5-ounce No. 4 load holds 203 pellets; if you had 165 hits in the 30-inch circle, the equation is 165x100 = 16,500 divided by 203 = .81, or 81 percent. The number of hits and percentage of hits are figures used for comparing the patterns of different loads. For an accurate comparison,

Comparative Retained Energy
Lead vs. Steel Shot

Shot Size	Metal	Muzzle Velocity	Retained Energy in Foot Pounds 40 Yds.	60 Yds.
No. 4	Steel	1,330 fps	2.4	1.3
No. 6	Lead	1,330 fps	2.3	1.3
No. 2	Steel	1,330 fps	4.3	2.6
No. 4	Lead	1,330 fps	4.4	2.7
BB	Steel	1,275 fps	8.3	5.2
No. 2	Lead	1,260 fps	7.0	4.6
T-Shot	Steel	1,350 fps	10.0 (50 Yds.)	8.5
No. 2	Lead	1,330 fps	5.7 (50 Yds.)	4.6

Source: SAMMI

This table assumes that the lead pellets remain round for optimum aerodynamics. If the lead pellets deform, their retained energies will be lower than the calculated values.

at least five shots from every load should be averaged. For easy future reference, write information about the gun, load, range, and pellet counts on the pattern sheets.

Lifesize Targets

To get an idea of how the pattern would actually strike waterfowl, use a lifesize duck or goose target. Some targets have a 30-inch circle to compare aim/impact points and to make pellet counts.

Lifesize targets show the accuracy of your pattern. Tight patterns do not allow much room for poor accuracy. If your gun doesn't shoot where you point, you might have to adjust your aim, do some gunsmithing, or replace the barrel or shotgun altogether.

The target also indicates how many pellets on average strike the vitals from a given load at a given yardage. Use this information to determine which loads give the best consistency and to learn your favorite load's range limitations.

Photo courtesy of R. L. Davis, Jr.

For close-range duck shooting, such as over decoys, steel 3 and 4 shot is recommended. Some hunters use steel 6s on small ducks, but current No. 6 loads seem to destroy meat on ducks too close and lose sufficient energy soon thereafter.

95

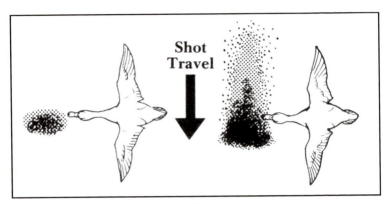

This exaggerated depiction of the difference between lead and steel shot patterns shows why shooters may score more fringe hits with lead. A wider and longer lead shot group, resulting from deformed pellets flying more slowly and erratically than the main charge, will account for a few more hits. The target may be hit by the edge of the generally wider lead pattern or by lagging lead pellets, whereas the narrower, shorter steel shot charge may have missed completely. While this characteristic of lead shot may result in a few more broken clay targets, it is not desirable for waterfowl hunting, in which fringe hits can cripple game.

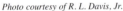

Photo courtesy of R. L. Davis, Jr.

Knowing your equipment and how to use it, is key when making waterfowling memories.

Determining Load Performance

What kind of performance is necessary from a shotgun load to bring down a duck or goose? Where does the line fall between shoot and don't shoot? All-encompassing answers to these questions do not exist because there are so many variables involved. But there are some general guidelines, the foremost being: If you're not sure, wait for a better shot.

Photo by Mike Strandlund

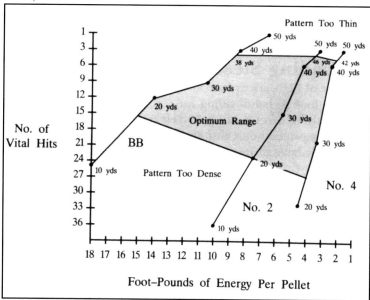

The effectiveness of a shotgun load is determined by its pellet energy and pattern density at the distances you shoot game. When shooting larger ducks, a minimum of four hits at the vitals with two foot-pounds of energy for each pellet is generally needed. The graph above indicates the optimum range for shooting ducks with different types of three-inch 12-gauge magnum loads. In this test, No. 2 shot showed the most consistency and the widest optimum range. Results will vary depending on gun, load, and conditions; perform your own tests before going hunting, using different shot sizes and chokes. Source: 1988 NRA Study

The main dilemma deals with pattern and range, specifically the number of pellets that must strike vital organs for a sure kill. As a general rule, each shot should deliver at least four or five pellets with sufficient energy for good penetration in the waterfowl's vital zone. (See graphs.) These figures are minimums, not averages; if you find that an occasional shot can't make these standards, try another load or shorten your range.

To determine your best load, select three or four likely loads and begin patterning one at 10 yards. Using the same load, increase your range by five yards for each group of shots, recording your results at each yardage. When you reach the point where your pattern becomes too sparse, you've gone beyond the maximum range for that load. Go through the same process with at least a couple other loads, and hunt with the one that gives the best results.

Pattern testing can be more interesting if you do it with a club or a few friends. You can help each other with problems or questions you may have, and a little friendly competition may lead to discovery of the best combination of gun and load for the best results.

Reloading Steel

Because of high prices for commercially loaded steel shot, many hunters look to hand loading for cost relief. This should not be done without careful, studious research into reliable literature, for loading steel shot is entirely different than loading lead shot. Steel loads have different "flow" characteristics than lead loads. Under the pressure of powder gasses, steel pellets bridge and present a virtual obstruction to forward wad movement, whereas lead pellets will compress and flow more readily from chamber to bore. Steel shot wedging in the chamber creates a lateral pressure that is easily seen in the deep "dimples" found in recovered shot cups. This unforgiving characteristic of steel shot necessitates special high-density plastic wads and powders with slow burning rates. One should never replace lead shot with steel shot to make use of leftover ammo, or vice versa. Nor should a hand loader ever use data and components for lead reloads for steel shot reloads, or vice versa. The pellet flow properties between the two metals have importantly different influences on chamber pressures, and mixing the two metals indiscriminately is like playing with dynamite. Do not assume you know anything about reloading steel shot until you've read in depth about the process and its potential pitfalls!

CHAPTER 6

GUNNING FOR WATERFOWL

ow far should I lead a duck? It's the first thing a beginning waterfowler wants to know, a legitimate question that brings a variety of answers. He'll be told in feet and in duck lengths just how far to lead that duck. But he'll learn the most not from a lecture, but from demonstration, trial, error, and success.

Good wingshooting deals with fundamentals and how to lead, not where to lead. Accomplished shotgunners often find they shoot better when they don't dwell too much on physics. They don't analyze the leads they use in hunting situations. They've learned through practice, through trial and error, to point, lead, and shoot instinctively.

The Fundamentals

The best way to learn shotgunning is to build a foundation of shotgun-handling skills and then learn through field experience to compute instantly and subconsciously all the factors that go into making a shot. These fundamentals include the following:

1) Stance
2) Gun-Ready Position
3) Swing to Target
4) Trigger Pull
5) Follow-Through

These steps are combined and refined for each specific situation to allow you to compensate for variations in shooting conditions, speed, angle, distance, and type of flight.

Determining Dominant Eye

Before you can develop your stance, you must decide whether to hold the gun to your right shoulder or your left. To do this, you must determine your dominant eye—the eye that sees the "strongest" image and the one you want to align with the bead and the target.

Photo courtesy of R. L. Davis, Jr.

After getting your shotgun basics down, practice shooting with positions and conditions you expect to have while hunting. Shooting while you're sitting or peeking through a blind can be quite different than the controlled conditions of a trap range.

To determine your dominant eye, cup your hands at arm's length with your palms facing away. Form a small hole between your hands and look through it to a distant object. Slowly draw your hands back toward your face, keeping the object in sight through the small gap between your hands. Your hands will naturally come back to one eye—this is your dominant eye. You should shoulder your shotgun on the same side as that eye.

Stance and Gun-Ready Position

Proper stance is the foundation of good shotgun shooting. It is essential as you develop a consistent shooting technique. The correct form keeps you well balanced and properly addressing your target. You are ready to raise the shotgun to the gun-ready position and rotate your body to follow the target's flight path. The right gun position allows smooth, quick mounting and the most accurate shooting.

When you're about to shoot, stand with your feet comfortably apart, about shoulder width, and with your body relaxed. Right-handed shooters should have their left foot forward in the direction they plan to shoot, with knees slightly bent, and leaning slightly forward. The proper shooting position is often compared to a boxer's stance. This position effectively points your body toward the target, reinforcing the concept of instinctive pointing, which will be extended through your arms and the shotgun.

Photo courtesy of R. L. Davis, Jr.

To achieve proper form, a right-handed shooter should spread his feet for good balance with his left foot forward; press the stock to his cheek and shoulder; hold the fore-end lightly in the most comfortable position; grip and control the gun with his right hand; keep his right elbow raised even with his right hand.

The shotgun should be held in front of the body with the butt about waist high and the muzzle slightly below eye level, pointing in the direction you plan to shoot. This position gives you clear view of the target area with the muzzle in your field of vision. Seeing both the bird and the muzzle adds to your ability to get on target.

101

Photos courtesy of M. Fleming

Some common mistakes in shotgun shooting form: If the head is lifted from the stock, shots tend to be high (top). Some beginners think the buttstock goes under the armpit, but after taking the recoil on the chin, seldom make the mistake again.

Grasp the gun's fore-end lightly—this promotes a smooth swing—and experiment to find a comfortable, consistent hold on the fore-end. Your hold on the stock's grip should be firm for utmost control in swinging and to help absorb recoil.

Photo courtesy of R. L. Davis, Jr.

Keeping your cheek pressed firmly on the stock, eyes focused on the target, is the most critical element of good shotgun shooting.

Swing to Target

When the target comes into view, focus your eyes on the bird as you bring the gun smoothly to your shoulder. It is important to concentrate and focus on the target, with just a peripheral awareness of the bead or muzzle; you're pointing rather than aiming. Maintain that concentration until after the shot.

It's best to keep both eyes open—for depth perception and a wider field of view—provided you shoulder your gun on the same side as your dominant eye. If you shoot from the shoulder opposite your dominant eye, you'll have problems shooting with both eyes open; the view down the barrel will not be the most distinct view. In this case, or if neither of your eyes is dominant, it's best to shoot with one eye closed.

As you begin to point the shotgun, bring the stock's butt away from your body and straight up, then back to meet your cheek with the butt pressed firmly against the "pocket" of your shoulder, which lies under your collar bone between your chest muscle and shoulder muscle. The top of the butt should be in line with the top of the shoulder. Avoid bringing your head down to meet the gun; this causes you to tilt your head, which makes sighting more difficult. Keep your cheek pressed against the stock—raising your head off the stock will raise your eye above the plane of the barrels, and you will tend to shoot high.

Determining Lead

A common mistake by beginning shotgunners is to shoot where the target is, rather than where it will be when the pellets arrive. They often fail to realize that it takes significant time for the shot to get there, and that there are several factors affecting lead.

These factors include:

- **Distance Between Shooter and Target**
- **Target Speed**
- **Reaction, Lock, and Ignition Times**
- **Shot Velocity**
- **Angle of Target Flight**
- **Muzzle Swing Speed**

The most significant factors are distance and the speeds of the target and shot. For example, consider a 35-yard crossing shot on a duck fly-

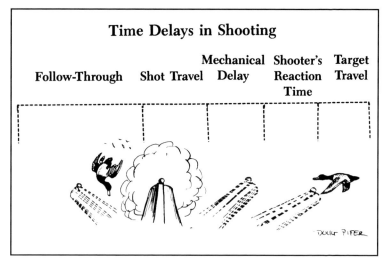

Time Delays in Shooting

Follow-Through	Shot Travel	Mechanical Delay	Shooter's Reaction Time	Target Travel

A shotgunner must adjust his lead to compensate for the time and distance factors affecting target and pattern. He must instantly, subconsciously compute target speed and angle, shooter reaction time, mechanical delay, shot travel time, and the speed of this follow through.

ing 40 miles per hour. The duck's speed translates to about 60 feet per second, compared with the average velocity of the shot at 1,000 feet per second. It will take your shot about one-tenth of a second to travel those 35 yards to the duck. In that same tenth of a second, the duck will have traveled six feet. To center the duck in the pattern, you will have to lead it by six feet, all other things being equal.

But remember, all things aren't always equal. There is also the angle of flight—if the duck is flying a bit toward or away from you, its lateral speed is reduced, and your lead must change correspondingly. Forward allowance (or lead) should be cut in half if the target is flying half as fast, is twice as close, or is angling at 45 degrees toward or away from you. Keep in mind reaction time—the time lapse between the instant your brain says, "pull the trigger" and you actually do pull the trigger. There is also the less significant lock time (time for your gun's mechanism to work) and ignition time (time it takes for the primer to go off, the powder to burn, and the pellets to travel down the barrel). These time lapses usually total about one-fifth of a second.

Obviously this is all too much to think about as you try to shoot a passing mallard. You have to learn through practice to calculate lead instantly, subconsciously. You must also take into consideration the type of swing you use.

Swing and Lead

There are three methods of swinging the muzzle and leading a target, with some slight variations. These methods include:

- **Swing-Through**
- **Sustained-Lead**
- **Snap-Shooting**

The swing-through method is the favorite of the great majority of trap competitors and is used by most hunters. It is usually the most natural and easiest-learned technique, and it encourages the shooter to follow through with muzzle swing—a critical element in most situations.

In the swing-through method, the shooter focuses on the target, swings the shotgun muzzle up from behind and past it, and begins to fire just before the correct lead is reached. Usually the trigger is pulled just as the shooter sees the muzzle has passed the target. There must be no hesitation nor change in the speed of the swing.

With swing-through, the shooter is not estimating the actual lead he needs; he leads through timing the trigger pull. Because of the reaction time lapse and the muzzle swinging faster than the target, the lead at the time of the shot is actually greater than it appears to the shooter.

Sustained Lead

Swing-Through

Snap Shooting

With sustained lead, the shooter maintains a constant forward allowance in front of his target, firing when he feels his swing and lead are right. The swing-through shooter brings the bead up from behind the target, passes it, and pulls the trigger when the lead appears right. Snap shooting—picking a spot where the pellet charge and target will intersect—is often best on suddenly flushed game or where shots must be threaded through timber.

With the sustained-lead technique, the shooter estimates the actual lead he needs and swings ahead of the target at about the same speed the target is traveling. At some point when he feels he has the proper lead and is swinging at the right speed, the shooter pulls the trigger. Because the lead remains more or less constant, reaction and lock times are not factors—provided the swing is smooth. Because the muzzle is not moving as fast as in the swing-through method, more forward allowance is needed for a sustained-lead.

In snap-shooting, there is no swing involved. The shooter directs the muzzle to a point in space where he believes the target and his shot pattern will meet, considering the comparative time lapse for each. Because the muzzle is not moving, significantly more lead is needed. There is also more room for error; any variation in lead or reaction time is magnified with this method, because the muzzle is not following the target.

Experts concur that swing-through is usually the easiest method to master. Most shooters adopt this style and stick with it most of the time, but hunting conditions often demand that you make changes. Usually, sustained lead is used in pass shooting, swing-through on closer shots, and snap-shooting on straightaways, on decoying ducks, and in timber where shots must be quick and threaded through openings in the branches. Whichever style of lead you use, practice with it thoroughly before you start shooting at game.

Trigger Pull

The quickness of winged targets demands that you shoot the instant you have a good sight picture. Shotgunners have to pull the trigger decisively, rather than squeeze it deliberately as a rifleman would. The trigger pull should be a subconscious reaction to seeing the proper sight picture. There may be a tendency to flinch, close your eyes, or slow your swing in anticipation of the blast. One way of avoiding these bad habits is to "call the shot."

Calling the shot consists of being fully conscious of what was happening the moment you pulled the trigger, so that you could "call" where your shot pattern hit in relation to the target. This not only gives you a good idea of where your shots are going, but also makes you more aware of flinching or hesitating the barrel swing. The mental picture you get of the moment you hit the trigger tells if you were holding high or low, where your lead was, and whether you made a smooth transition between swing and follow-through.

Follow-Through

The most common cause of missing is shooting behind the target. The most common reason for this is prematurely stopping the swing. Some shotgunners have a natural tendency of stopping the swing at the moment they pull the trigger, almost as if it were physically impossible to swing and pull the trigger at the same time. But it's a habit that must be broken for consistent shooting.

Follow-through means continuing the swing until well after the shot is fired. It assures that the proper lead is reached with the swing-through method or maintained with the sustained-lead swing during the reaction, lock, and ignition sequence.

Shooting Steel

Some shooters believe steel shot requires minor adjustments in the amount of forward allowance needed at various ranges. Although steel pellets do slow down quicker than lead shot of the same size and shape, they are usually faster inside their initial 25-35 yards of flight due to (1) their spherical shape for optimum aerodynamics and (2) their relatively high muzzle velocities (steel loads usually have muzzle velocities above 1,350 feet per second, to ensure as high an energy as possible within the parameters of safe chamber pressures). Within those first 25-35 yards, therefore, some shooters believe slightly shorter leads may be mandated.

In the midrange area of 30-45 yards, steel shot slows more than lead to compensate for its initial higher velocity. But as range increases beyond 45 yards, aerodynamic factors work against steel shot to suggest longer leads than those for lead shot. Of course, there are some variations based on individual pellet sizes and load velocity. The heavier steel BBBs and T-shot retain their velocities better than steel 2s, 4s, and 6s.

The differences in proper leads for steel and lead loads is not as great as many hunters have been led to believe, however. Some feel that the difference in velocity and deceleration plays havoc with their shooting style, and claim they have to totally revamp their leads. But when the ballistics are examined, it appears the difference has little significance, as illustrated here.

(Because velocities vary greatly according to each load's powder charge and shot charge weights, precise calculations are not possible for overall comparisons of steel and lead shot. The following examples approximate the factors involved in leading a target flying at a 90-degree angle to the shotgun barrel. Differences in forward allowance would be less for other angles.)

The vital zone on a waterfowl is much smaller than the bird appears. Usually at least three or four hits—within the energy range of the pellet—are needed to bring the game down immediately.

Most lead shot loads leave the muzzle at about 1,250 feet per second, compared to 1,350 for steel shot—about an 8 percent difference. At 20 yards, because steel is slowing faster than lead, steel shot reaches the target about 5 percent sooner than lead shot. How much does this affect your forward allowance? A target traveling at a 90-degree angle 40 miles per hour covers about three feet in the time it takes shot pellets to get the 20 yards from the muzzle to the target. The 5 percent difference in velocity, divided into that three feet of required lead, translates to a forward allowance difference of less than two inches. That difference is hardly significant when compared to a pattern diameter of 30 inches or so. Even expert shotgunners cannot point a shotgun with that degree of precision.

At 35-45 yards, steel and lead arrive at the target at about the same time, so there should be no actual difference at that range. This is the distance where most waterfowl is shot, so lead/steel forward allowance concerns have no bearing whatsoever on the large portion of duck and goose shooting.

Beyond that range, steel sheds velocity faster and gets to the target a bit later than lead. How much later? Even if you were shooting at 50 yards, which is beyond waterfowl-shooting range, you could figure a difference of less than 5 percent. (Remember, because you are using larger pellet sizes with steel, the velocity difference will not be as great as with steel and lead pellets of equal size. Also, steel pellets retain their roundness and have less air drag than slightly deformed lead shot.) The target will have traveled about 14 feet in the time it takes for the shot to get there, assuming an average velocity of a little over 800 fps. Five percent or less of this 14 feet is less than an eight-inch difference in forward allowance (more likely two to four inches)—again insignificant compared to a pattern diameter of 50 inches or more.

If you are accustomed to using high-velocity lead loads, with muzzle velocity around 1,330 fps, you may notice a difference in required forward allowance for steel at maximum ranges. Express lead loads may get to a long-range target significantly sooner than one of the slower steel loads.

The differences in velocity, again, will vary from load to load, proportionally affecting forward allowance. Actually, the velocity variance between different lead loads can be greater than the difference between certain lead and steel loads. With lead waterfowl loads, a smaller powder charge pushing a heavier pellet charge may average only about 1,200 fps, while a heavier powder charge and light shot load may start at over 1,400 fps. In these cases, shooters should note greater differences in required forward allowance between different lead loads than between some lead and steel loads.

If a shooter does have difficulty hitting targets with steel, it is probably a reflection of the tighter pattern and shorter shot string he has to work with. Or the problem could relate to attitude rather than physics. Confidence and mental approach play a pivotal role in shooting success. If a shooter expects to do poorly with steel, or is preoccupied with changing his lead, he is likely to lose his concentration, make a minor change in technique, and miss.

When to Shoot?

A frequent dilemma facing the waterfowler is when to shoot. In some situations, the answer is fairly clear. Jump shooters fire immediately, as long as the target is well within range. Pass shooters should wait until the duck or goose has reached the closest point and will begin gaining yardage—again, provided it is in range. Hunters luring waterfowl with calls or decoys should let birds approach to very close range, if possible, until the target is flying low and slow.

But what about those frustrating times when ducks or geese circle or buzz by in marginal range? Knowing when to shoot and when to wait is a sense that sets expert waterfowlers apart. It is acquired only with experience.

Some species like pintails and snow geese are well known for taking their time dropping to a set. Often a hunter will hold for a closer shot as a flock buzzes by within range, then watch helplessly as they leave, never to be seen again. The only answer here is to base judgments on experience - best of all on experience from earlier that day. If you decide the game will probably not approach any closer, your best shot may be a difficult shot. But here, the cardinal rule applies: Make sure it is in range.

Estimating Range

To tell whether a bird is in range and to estimate lead, you have to be a fair judge of distance. It may help somewhat to step off and study various yardages in the field, but the ranges of fast-flying ducks can be deceptive.

One general rule to follow is that when flying at 40 yards, medium-sized ducks like mallards usually appear as long as a shotgun muzzle appears wide. If it looks significantly smaller, it is probably out of

Here's a general rule of estimating range: A mallard appearing the same width as your 12-gauge shotgun muzzle is at about 40 yards, or at the edge of effective shooting range. A similar-sized duck that appears smaller than your gun's muzzle is out of range. If you use this system, remember to keep your focus on the duck and compare the muzzle in your peripheral vision.

range. (This does not suggest changing your focus from target to gun muzzle. You should be able to make a size comparison with just a peripheral view of your muzzle.)

To test this rule and get a look from various yardages, you can use a dead duck or life size decoy. Place the target on the ground or hang it up, step off various distances, and point your shotgun at the target. Make a mental picture of the relative sizes of the bird and your muzzle at the different ranges.

You can also use decoys, trees, or other landmarks at known distances to measure range. Some hunter education instructors inflate duck-size balloons with helium, and have students estimate their range. Frequently guessing and then stepping off yardage to landmarks in the woods also helps your range estimation.

Improving Shotgun Skills

Practice and experimentation is the only way for the waterfowl shot-gunner to reach a high level of skill. This skill should be developed on clay targets at a practice range, not on game in the field.

Trap and skeet ranges are the typical places for shotgunners to experiment with different shooting styles and to hone their skills. Even better are hunter's clays ranges, where clay targets present shots that more closely resemble those offered by waterfowl. It is best to practice with the loads you'll hunt with, if it is allowed at the range.

If you don't have these facilities available, you can get good practice with a hand trap or even thrown targets. Practice-pointing, dry-firing, and visualization of shooting can improve your skill, even when you can't actually shoot.

Practicing for the Hunt

After learning and practicing with the "classic" shotgunner's stance, practice shooting under the conditions of waterfowl hunting. Shoot sitting on a seat, as if in a boat; kneeling, as if in a small shoreline blind; pointing through a small opening, as if in a box or pit blind; even sitting on the ground, as if in a lay-out blind or boat. Keep in mind the type of hunting you plan to do, and simulate those conditions. This includes the lighting and clothing you expect to have while hunting.

Part III

How To Hunt
Ducks And Geese

Photo courtesy of Wayne Gendron

Photo courtesy of P. Giarth

CHAPTER 7

SETTING UP THE WATERFOWL HUNT

S ome of the very best waterfowling takes place in backyards and easy chairs, over lunch counters and telephone lines, by a lake on an August afternoon. For some people, the only thing better than waterfowl hunting is *getting ready* for waterfowl hunting. Preparation is not only the key to successful duck and goose hunting. It is an enjoyable pastime with exciting anticipation and fond stories of hunts past as you plan more for the future.

The amount of preseason work you have to do depends on your experience, familiarity with the area, and your approach to waterfowl hunting, be it simple or complex. There are four basic areas of waterfowl hunting preparation:

- **Studying Waterfowl and Hunting**
- **Learning About Local Ducks and Geese**
- **Building Blinds**
- **Preparing Equipment**

Educating Yourself

The first step is to learn as much as possible about hunting waterfowl. If you are relatively new to the sport, this is critical. You should spend as much time reading, talking, and listening about waterfowl as you can. If you're an expert, you probably realize more each year how much you *don't* know about waterfowl, and upgrading your knowledge and skill is an annual thing.

Read books and magazine articles. Even the most experienced hunters can learn an extra trick or bit of valuable information every time they pick up literature on the subject. To further understand the game you pursue, read or reread a good waterfowl natural history book such as *Ducks, Geese, and Swans of North America* by Frank Bellrose, published by Stackpole Books and the Wildlife Management Institute.

Stay up to date by studying the annual fall flight reports published by the U.S. Fish and Wildlife Service, and the hunting regulations pub-

Photo courtesy of M. Embrey

Preparation is often the key to success and enjoyment in waterfowling.

lished by your state. These can provide insight to which species are up, which are down, and when and where to hunt.

Joining a club such as the local Ducks Unlimited chapter, and attending seminars, can put you in contact with other hunters who can impart valuable know-how. Hunter clinics, such as the Waterfowl Hunter Clinic Program conducted by the National Rifle Association, provide you with valuable information; so do video and audio tapes on the subject.

Some of this knowledge takes special application to your personal situation. For example, you can learn how ducks are called, but you'll have to practice a lot to do it yourself. You may develop a mental picture of the perfect blind site, but you'll have to do the footwork to actually find it.

Scouting Habitat and Patterning: Waterfowl

To put general knowledge to work, hunters have to apply it to the specific areas and birds they hunt.

If you are new to an area, start with contacting the local wildlife manager or game department. They can give information on the best public areas and maybe some likely prospects for getting permission on private land.

Sometimes that is the only contact needed, but talking with other hunters and landowners themselves can yield information on the best local "hotspots."

Maps are also very valuable to pinpoint those out-of-the-way duck magnets. They show bodies of water and wetlands, public hunting areas, access points, and roads. Plat books name property owners, and topographic maps show the most details and land contours.

Once you have likely spots located, you have to do on-site scouting. This helps you assess resident populations of waterfowl and identify feeding places, loafing areas, roosting sites, and flight patterns between each. You should also monitor water levels and make note of grain fields where waterfowl might feed after harvest. It is much easier to decoy waterfowl where they feed rather than trying to divert them from their flight pattern.

Patterning should be done during the same times as hunting: the first two and last two hours of daylight, when waterfowl fly most. Some of the favorite locations of flyways are along rivers, in a straight line between two smaller bodies of water, between a large big-water resting area and shallow feeding area. Often times, waterfowl avoid places that can hide hunters, especially later in the season. They prefer to fly across the middle of large bodies of water rather than skirt shorelines. For this reason, islands and points sticking out into these bodies of water are often close to flyways.

While geography provides some ideas on locating flyways, the only sure bet is to get out and observe the waterfowl. Some puddlers, such as wood ducks, flock at dusk to a certain pothole, while a nearly identical pond a couple hundred yards away will sit empty of ducks. Geese may fly over a dozen harvested cornfields, then land in a nondescript flat of yellow stubble.

These waterfowl pockets change as hunting pressure increases or feed is exhausted. They must be scouted regularly during the season. Find where waterfowl feed or rest by driving or walking around all the potential waterways. Glass them from a distance to keep from spooking any birds that might be there. While scouting big water, make sure to check all the bays where flocks could be secluded. Scout at different times of day, and if it's during the season, hunt a flock as soon as you find it. It may not be there more than a day or two.

If you're hunting geese in crop fields, try to set up several hunting sites. Don't use the same blind more than twice a week. Locate areas geese are using by searching high spots in fields for droppings and preened feathers.

Goose hunters often locate current feeding sites by spotting a flock as it leaves roost on a refuge or big water, then following the flock by car until it lands to feed. Then the hunters try to get permission to hunt the field and return well before daybreak to set up. The geese may return right on schedule—or never be seen again.

Blind Sites and Construction

Scouting is for more than just locating birds; it should tell you exactly where to set up. Don't make the mistake of building a blind a little ways off the flyway, in a more convenient place, with hopes that passing ducks will spot your decoys and veer from their predetermined path. That happens for only the most experienced decoyers and callers. Most waterfowlers must hunt at a feeding or resting site, or under the flyway for consistent success.

When selecting a blind site, keep these points in mind:

- **Ducks and geese will try to land only where they want to; no amount of decoys or expert calling will convince them to land at an unfavorable location. The blind site should be a good, *natural* landing site.**
- **Wind and sun should be at your back. Waterfowl land into the wind, and sun behind you helps your eyesight while hindering that of the birds.**
- **Try to find a site with the right amount of cover. Too little, and you may have a hard time hiding or have to build a conspicuous blind. Too much, and wary birds may avoid the site for fear of hidden predators.**

Photo courtesy of M. Fleming

A big box or piano blind is roomy and comfortable, allowing hunters to move around.

Even if you're sure of your blind site, avoid building a permanent blind right away. It's best to hunt from a temporary blind your first few times in the area. It can save a lot of time and money if you find the ducks ignoring you and passing 300 yards away. Test the area using a temporary set-up the first season, and you'll know where to put your fancy blind next year.

Portable Blinds

Temporary or portable blinds may not be as comfortable as the more solid bunkers with seats and roofs, but they can be quite effective and

119

allow you to move easily as the unpredictable flocks of waterfowl change their flight and feeding patterns. Temporary blinds generally fit into three categories:

- **Natural Hides**
- **Commercial or Homemade Portable Blinds**
- **Boat Blinds**

The simplest blind is the type you don't have to set up and never leave: camouflaged clothing and equipment. It can also be one of the most effective. A motionless hunter in good camouflage, with matching background and perhaps a leafy limb overhead, can be practically invisible to waterfowl.

Good camouflage means head to toe and the correct type to match the surroundings. While color doesn't make much difference with game like deer, ducks and geese see color better than humans. Make sure you don't have a white T-shirt sticking out at your neck or shiny buckles to give you away. Cover your hands with gloves and shade your face with a big-billed cap. You may want to use a headnet—a full-face headnet if you wear glasses.

The waterfowl hunter without a blind must make use of all available cover, of course. Don't forget the concealing ability of the water itself with chest waders, a hunter can hide nearly half his body underwater.

Big rivers—natural flyways that attract many ducks—offer good, natural blinds. One of the best is made by digging a kneedeep hole in a sandbar where ducks stop to preen, rest, and gather gravel. Place driftwood around the hole, step in, and lie on your back. You will be virtu-

Photo courtesy of R. L. Davis, Jr.

A small shoreline hide is often the best blind—quick to set up, take down, and move.

ally invisible if you are wearing wood-pattern camouflage, yet be able to see well and stand quickly to shoot.

The next simplest blind is a portable cover. Hunters have used old burlap bags and similar scavenged material for decades. Today there are several makes of portable blinds on the market offering a leafy, three-dimensional hide that is quite effective.

Some of these covers are sold with frames, but they are usually just suspended from a couple of limbs or stakes. In timber, a camo cover hung from a branch is sufficient; on a snowy, icy shoreline, a couple of stakes suspending an old bed sheet can make surprisingly good camouflage.

Photo courtesy of R. L. Davis, Jr.

A simple yet effective shoreline blind can be built with a few stakes and a large piece of camouflaged cloth.

Goose hunters find these covers ideal for their type of hunting, in which the wary waterfowl are suspicious of any object on a field. Some Canada goose hunters lay in a field of decoys with just a good camouflaged cover over themselves. A favorite tactic of snow goose hunters is to lie under a white sheet that blends with a field full of white goose decoys.

Photos courtesy of M. Fleming

Photos courtesy of R. L. Davis, Jr.

Boat blinds have many advantages over permanent blinds or temporary hides. They provide versatility and mobility, and allow hunters to hide among an open-water spread for wary divers. Disadvantages: They are usually less comfortable and more conspicuous.

Boat Blinds

Hunters who travel by watercraft to their hunting sites often turn their boat into a blind. This accomplishes two tasks: it provides a comfortable, moveable blind, and eliminates the need to hide your boat after reaching your hunting site. You just park, throw out the decoys, and wait for the ducks.

Boat blinds range from a simple dull-painted, grassed-over canoe to a large johnboat with a fancy built-on box blind. A common compromise is a camouflage-painted boat and large camo cover that allows hunters to sit on the seats and still remain concealed. "Grassing" the boat with a few armfuls of vegetation from the blind site adds an effective finishing touch.

Some hunters with large, stable boats construct take-down blinds consisting of small panels. Usually made of grass-thatched chicken wire and light wood or aluminum frames, they are stacked for easy transport. At the hunting site, they are assembled and bolted to the boat in ten minutes or so.

In all such blinds, the boat must be secured for safety and to keep it from bobbing in the waves and spooking ducks. You might clamp it to stakes or wire it to shoreline shrubs. The boat should appear like an extension of the shoreline, if possible. If it must be set in open water, brush it up well and scatter decoys all around it. Place smaller pieces of brush around the boat, also. This makes the boat appear to be an island surrounded by smaller islands.

The layout boat is a low-profile craft that, instead of resembling a clump of marsh grass, is designed to blend in with the water. Hunters lie under a cover amid a decoy spread waiting for birds to near. This type of hunting usually requires a bigger backup boat, waiting nearby, in case the small vessel should capsize or swamp.

Permanent Blinds

Another type of boat blind is more aptly termed a boathouse blind. It is a camouflaged slip that hides the boat and its occupants. It is constructed of driven posts and a framework that typifies permanent blinds.

Permanent blinds are more comfortable than portable set-ups. In some areas they also let the user license a blind site, which keeps other hunters from moving in on the area. They take time to build, however, and are not allowed in all areas.

The favorite permanent blinds among duck hunters are box or piano blinds. Construction starts with four or six posts, forming the corners

Photo courtesy of R. L. Davis, Jr.

Pit blind construction can be an elaborate affair, employing backhoes and concrete liners. The time and money spent pays off in comfort and durability.

and maybe center supports, driven solidly into firm soil. A frame of boards or poles is nailed or wired to the posts and covered with plywood or chickenwire. Grass, branches, small cedar trees, and such conceal the carpentry and blend the blind with its surroundings. Some hunters leave the top open, but best success comes with at least a partial concealing roof.

Photo courtesy of M. Fleming

Waterfowlers must be well camouflaged if they hunt from a blind that does not provide total concealment.

In designing and positioning the blind, consider shooting situations. Try to build the blind away from trees that retreating ducks could use as cover. Face it toward your decoy area but construct the blind so you can also shoot behind, if possible. If you hunt with a retriever, make a platform for him to watch the action. When a dog can see the duck drop, the retrieve is much smoother and faster.

A variation of the box blind is the stilt blind, most popular in big-water areas. Usually large and raised on pilings offshore, a stilt blind's indiscreet presence makes it less effective for the more wary birds. They are used mainly for gunning divers and sea ducks.

Another type of permanent blind is the pit blind dug into a field. These also range from rough to fancy, from one-man dirt depressions dug just before the hunt, to elaborate six-man, concrete-lined bunkers. They are usually used for goose hunting.

The function of a permanent pit blind is to offer the comforts of a box blind but with nearly complete concealment of hunters and the blind itself. To maximize this, most pit blind hunters make a half-roof with well-camouflaged pop-off or sliding panels over the shooting slot. Dirt dug from the pit should be removed or spread out, and the ground around the blind should not be trampled or otherwise conspicuous.

125

Photo courtesy of R. L. Davis, Jr.

A good field pit blind is comfortable and well away from trees and brush, as geese are often shy of landing near structure that could hide hunters. The blind should offer total concealment—in this case light covers that are tossed away when the shooting begins.

Photo courtesy of R. L. Davis, Jr.

One man "layout" blinds have become increasingly popular and offer major concealment and mobility.

Field blinds for geese should be built on the highest part of the field, where good visibility gives geese a sense of security. Toward the end of season, however, geese may have eaten all the feed in the center of the field and be working the edges. Place your blinds accordingly.

Other Blinds

Many other types of blinds have been used by waterfowl gunners. Perhaps the most successful was the old-time sink box made famous by East Coast market hunters. Sink boxes were watertight barrels or boxes

127

that effectively hid the hunter underwater. Only a small lip stuck above the waterline to keep the blind from flooding. They were so effective that they have been outlawed by the U.S. government.

Build blinds well before hunting season so local birds get used to their presence. You may want to spend more time scouting and finalizing details as opening day approaches. In the interim, your attention should turn toward getting your equipment in order.

Photo courtesy of R. L. Davis, Jr.

Hunters should take the time to pattern their shotgun. Life-size game targets make patterning a shotgun easy and fun.

Photo courtesy of R. L. Davis, Jr.

Before the hunting season, make sure firearms are in good working order.

Gear Preparation

It's best to get your equipment, yourself, and your dog ready well before the season. It can be a big job, especially if you want to use a boat or big decoy rig. Starting early also helps you remember the small details that can mean the difference between a successful hunt or total failure.

Here are some equipment preparation points to remember:

- Make sure your boat, motor, and trailer are in good repair. Touch up the boat's paint and repair leaks, broken oar locks, burned-out

129

running lights, etc. Stow life jackets and other necessary boating equipment. Tune up the motor. Make sure the trailer has a spare tire and working lights.

- Touch-up the paint on decoys; replace those lost or destroyed. Replace anchors and lines if necessary.
- Patch hip boots and waders.
- Get all licenses, including duck stamps (signed and attached to your license), boat registration, and trailer license plate.
- Pattern shotguns and practice shooting.
- Make sure calls are in good working condition.
- Work with your dog to brush up retrieving skills—both his and yours.

Knowing which calls to have and how to use them is an important part of pre-season preparation.

Photo courtesy of R.L. Davis, Jr.

CHAPTER 8

DECOYS AND THEIR DEPLOYMENT

A good decoy spread not only attracts waterfowl, it puts them where you want them. More than anything else, the art of waterfowl hunting is knowing how and where to drop your decoys. This art takes many forms as hunters select color and proportion in their blocks, design decoy patterns on the waters, sculpt areas where the properly fooled duck or goose will drop its feet. Some waterfowlers believe a decoy rig should be intricate and as perfect as possible, while others see beauty in a simple pattern.

Photo courtesy of R.L. Davis, Jr.

Well-placed decoys bring the birds in close right in front of the blind. Shots at decoying birds, flying slow and low, are among the easiest.

Through scores of seasons, many decoying theories and systems have been developed. Some emerged more successful than others and became the old standbys. But sometimes one will work, another time it may not. You have to match your decoying to the place you hunt, the way you hunt, and the birds you hunt, to get *them* to come hunting *you*.

Decoying Basics

A century ago, waterfowlers had better decoys and calls to work with than they do today. That's because the decoys were real ducks making real calls. This method proved a little too successful, though, and responsible hunters realized they could conserve ducks and have more sport with counterfeit birds and calls. With lots of ducks and fewer hunters, decoying back then was easy. But generations of learning have taught waterfowl to be more wary. Today, hunters need lots of good decoys in a good arrangement to convince waterfowl to lower their landing gear.

The science of decoying waterfowl consists of decoy location, pattern, type, number, and placement.

Location of Decoys

Location of the decoy spread is critical for several reasons. The basic rule is to keep the sun, wind, and right amount of cover at your back.

Flocks must first of all be able to see your spread. If the decoys are hidden by a high bank, trees, or other obstructions, they are useless. The spread must be close enough to the blind that ducks or geese are not prone to landing out of shotgun range. Decoyed waterfowl will invariably try to land into the wind, so hunters can usually predict their angle of approach. Decoys can be located so ducks attempt to land just as they get past the shooters, which sets up the best shot—when birds are closest and flying slowest. On the other hand, if decoys are located improperly, birds may land outside your shooting zone. Or, they may fly by one end of the blind and deny most of the blind occupants a chance to shoot.

Ideally, the decoys should be set so that hunters are between the decoying birds and the sun. This hinders the game's sight defenses while helping you shoot better, and also makes it easier to identify game species and sex.

Pattern of Decoys

The pattern of your decoy set is also vital in attracting birds and luring them to where you want them to land. Most patterns have an opening or pocket facing downwind where the decoying birds should land. These patterns are often described as C, V, and J patterns, after their shape as seen from above. Fancy, complex patterns are not generally more effective, except that they may give hunters more confidence and keep them sitting still longer.

The opening or pocket should be well within shotgun range and encourage the most ideal angle of approach. There should be no decoys downwind of the opening because waterfowl are sometimes reluctant to make a low landing approach over sitting birds. The outside edge of the spread should also be within range, so that ducks that opt to land there are legitimate targets.

Numbers of Decoys

In most waterfowling, the amount of waterfowl you will attract is proportional to the amount of decoys you have. As waterfowl get more and more wise to the ways of hunters, it takes more and more decoys to convince them it's safe to land. And with more hunters using big rigs these days, you will need a bigger rig to compete for the game's attention.

The big-rig rule doesn't apply in all cases, however. Small openings in flooded timber need few decoys; small bunches look more natural. Hunting the wary black duck, you may have more success using two or three decoys than using more.

Type of Decoys

The size, shape, and color of the decoys you use can affect success. Try to use decoys matching the same species you're hunting. *Always* use puddle duck decoys for puddle ducks and divers for divers. If you're not sure about the species you'll be hunting, go by this rule: Select puddle duck decoys if you hunt marshes, timber, and potholes. Buy diver duck decoys if you hunt big water.

If you can't afford different rigs, "generic" decoys often work. While waterfowl are sometimes decoyed with objects as unlikely as newspapers and mud piles, the most detailed, realistic contours and paint will get the best results. You can add a few less realistic blocks to enlarge your set.

Larger, "magnum" style decoys are increasingly popular because birds can see them from farther away. They are also more expensive, however, which leads to a question: Should a hunter with limited cash buy magnum decoys or more of the smaller decoys? Most experienced waterfowlers believe *more* decoys are better than *bigger* decoys. Most hunters feel free to mix decoys of different sizes, while some advise against it.

Placement of Decoys

The way you set blocks is important in several ways. Most decoy spreads work best if dekes are set in groups of three to five, resembling family units. Don't set them too closely or let them touch; this simulates an alarmed flock ready to take flight. Make sure no blocks are tipped and showing their undersides or anchor strings. If you use decoys representing different species, keep all blocks of the same species together. Always set the most realistic-looking decoys on the downwind side of the spread, as these blocks will be eyed most carefully as birds approach

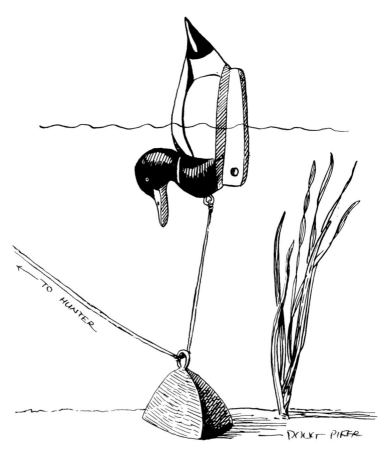

A tipping decoy, made with a standard deke and operated with a line and anchor system, adds realism and attractive movement to your set.

Photo courtesy of M. Fleming

Puddle ducks are normally more wary than divers, fooled only by realistic rigs of realistic decoys.

from that direction. When calling, always keep at least one decoy close to your blind. Sometimes waterfowl can pinpoint the sound, and they may spook if they don't see a decoy there.

Anchors and Rigging

Floating decoys must be secured to keep them from drifting and ruining the pattern. This is accomplished with anchors—either individual weights for each decoy or several decoys attached together and to a single anchor.

The best anchor line for individual decoys is a strong, dark-colored, specially made decoy line. It may be treated to prevent rot. The next best is monofilament of at least 15-pound test, though this tangles easily. Do not use light-colored cord, as this can be quite visible to descending waterfowl.

Ideally, each decoy should be equipped with just enough line to reach bottom on the deepest waters you hunt. When you hunt shallower areas, wrap surplus line around the deke's keel and tie it off.

The best single-decoy anchors are lead strips or rings. With the first type, the anchor line is wrapped around the decoy and the anchor is pinched over the wraps to hold them in place. With the ring type, line is wrapped around the anchor and the anchor is slipped over the decoy's head. They both serve to make the package neat and easy to handle.

Tying dekes together with thicker rope allows you to handle more decoys faster. Up to a dozen decoys per line can be managed by a single hunter, and some big operations can handle more. Make sure the line is camouflaged and has sufficient weight at each end to keep the line taut between decoys. Concrete blocks or bricks are often necessary.

Decoying Puddle Ducks

The most popular type of waterfowling is decoying puddle ducks — mainly mallards, pintails, teal, and wood ducks—on small bodies of water.

Puddle ducks are usually more wary than divers, so a realistic spread is important. Puddlers gather randomly, in small bunches, so your decoys should too.

In flooded timber, find an opening large enough that passing birds can see your spread easily. If possible, set up on the upwind side of the opening so decoying ducks will tend to fly at you over the water.

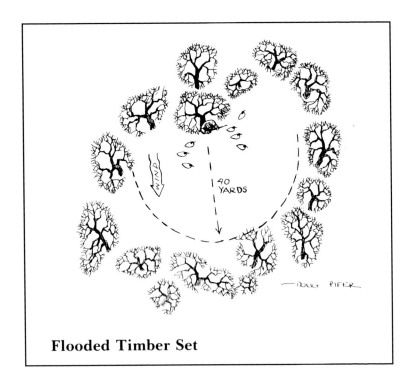

Flooded Timber Set

Set the decoys—from two to two dozen—on either side of your blind. This encourages the ducks to land in the opening directly in front of you.

Blinds are usually not necessary for hunting in timber. Most hunters simply dress in camouflage and break up their outline by leaning against a tree trunk.

A hunter concealed and standing in water can add realistic sound and movement to his set. Kicking the water surface depicts the commotion of feeding ducks. The sound can attract ducks as a feeding call would, and the ripples moving through the spread add sight attraction.

On bigger water, more decoys should be used. Most hunters group at least a dozen decoys on each side of their blind, with an opening in the center, or set them in a C pattern with the opening facing downwind. With two or more hunters, an effective pattern is the figure 8, with hunters spread out in front of the openings.

Photo courtesy M. Embrey

Smaller coves are often the best places to rig out around big water, especially if the weather is turning rough.

If the weather is rough, ducks seek shelter. Coves are then the best places to hunt on big water. Find a bay with the breeze from behind or from one side. Set the decoys in two groups or in a C shape, with the opening directly in front of the blind and facing downwind.

Divers are known for their willingness to decoy. Several species can be attracted to your well thought out spread.

The classic diver duck formation, the J or fishhook pattern, can also be effective on puddlers and other waterfowl. The long shank of the fishhook, pointing downwind, serves as an attention getter, with decoys strung out 60 yards or so. Once attracted, waterfowl should be convinced to land by a concentration of decoys at the bend of the fishhook, right in front of the blind. This pattern works best with the wind coming from behind the blind or along the shoreline. If the wind comes from across the water, ducks will offer difficult shots at best. At worst, they may avoid the set because landing is difficult or because they are shy of flying low over the shore.

Most puddle duck hunters use one type of decoy—usually mallard replicas. This reflects the fact that both mallards and mallard decoys are the most abundant of their kind. It works because the various species of puddle ducks intermingle frequently.

Some hunters believe in using other species, however. On large rafts of decoys, adding a few dekes of a different type adds a touch of realism. Some hunters, especially on the Atlantic Flyway, use mostly black duck decoys. Black ducks, most common in this region, are among the wariest waterfowl. Hunters often need well-made, well-placed black duck decoys to fool these birds. Other waterfowl, knowing the black's shrewd nature, may decoy better to a black duck rig than to another type.

This "confidence" effect can also be produced by using decoys resembling geese or shorebirds.

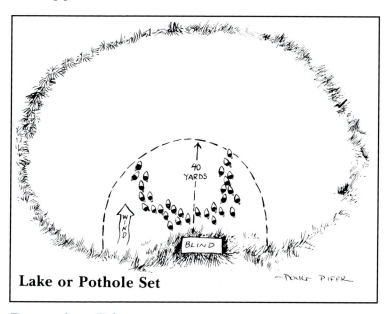

Lake or Pothole Set

Decoying Divers

While puddle duck hunting is characterized by small water and relatively small decoy spreads, diver duck hunting means big water and big rigs.

Divers as a rule are not as spooky as puddle ducks. Rather than striving for a natural, randomly spaced spread, diver hunters make bolder rigs designed for high visibility and pulling ducks close. Rigs are commonly 100 or more blocks, laid out in strings or elongated J patterns.

Photo courtesy M. Fleming

For divers, use large decoy spreads, in big water.

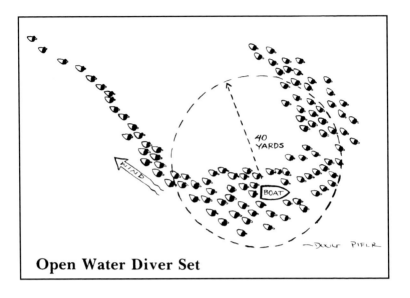

Open Water Diver Set

Diver ducks relate to and follow geographic contours, such as underwater drop-offs or weed lines. Therefore it is natural for decoys to be set in lines, and natural for decoyed divers to follow these lines — theoretically, to the hunter.

The most common set for divers is the J, or fishhook, pattern mentioned earlier. The shank of the hook is extended 100 yards or more into the water with decoys set more sparsely at the far end. These decoys are attractors that draw fast-flying divers toward the pattern's bend. Toward the bottom of the bend, the pattern gets more dense and helps distract the flock's attention from the boat or blind. The hunter should be hidden near the point of the hook and pick his shots as the birds try to land inside the bend. Some hunters set up away from smaller decoy patterns, about 35-40 yards, to be less visible. With this set, the more decoys the better.

Another good diver set, again exploiting their tendency to follow strings of decoys, is the V pattern. Strings of diver decoys, about 100 yards long, are set in a V formation. The blind and biggest concentration of decoys are at the bottom of the V, which points into the wind. Make sure the pattern is more dense at the tip of the V, to encourage birds to land close to the blind and not at the opening of the formation.

Divers seek security by winging out over open water and avoiding shorelines. Diver gunners therefore have best success with their rigs out in open water. Not expecting danger in the open, divers are much less wary than puddlers and decoy readily. In fact, the sea ducks are so bold

Photos courtesy of Mighty Layout Boys, LLC.

Big-water rigs for divers, such as scaup, often utilize layout boats. Hunters can take turns gunning from the layout boat and using a tender boat to retrieve ducks.

they can be lured to an uncamouflaged boat with a crude spread of black-painted milk jugs.

While most divers will decoy to any diver decoys, you can increase your odds by using decoys of the species you encounter.

Among the "Big Three" of divers—canvasbacks, scaup, and red-heads—canvasbacks tend to be the most wary. They, more than the others respond best to decoys of their own kind. For this reason, and because the white-backed blocks are very visible, canvasback decoys are usually best for divers.

Goldeneyes, buffleheads, and ruddy ducks also decoy best to blocks of their own kind, though they often come to any diver rig. The ringneck is in a group all its own; while it is classed as a diver, it feeds in shallows with puddle ducks. Hunters who want to shoot ringnecks sometimes put a few ringneck blocks alongside their puddle duck spread, though these birds are often shot over other big-water diver rigs.

Combination Decoy Sets

Hunting along the shoreline of bigger water—especially points on large lakes—you may encounter both divers and puddle ducks. You can set two decoy rigs and have a chance of gunning both types of ducks. Make sure to use both puddler and diver decoys and keep the two groups separate. In nature, the two types may feed next to each other, but they don't usually intermingle. Also, incoming birds can more easily identify with blocks of their own type if the decoys are segregated.

This is the most popular combination set for both puddlers and divers: From a shoreline or shallow water blind, extend a long string of diver decoys out into the water. Close to shore, set them about six feet

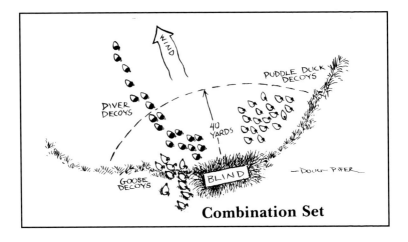

Combination Set

apart and on one side of your blind. On the other side, set a smaller spread of puddle duck decoys. These should be more spaced than the diver dekes, as natural flocks usually are. In open-water hunting, set two J or fishhook patterns.

Mallards often feed in fields and will decoy to a goose spread on the field. You can encourage this by setting a separate mallard rig to one side of your goose blocks.

Decoying Canada Geese

Among the wariest waterfowl, Canada geese look over a decoy spread closely, invariably circling several times, before coming in or flying off. But careful rigs and good decoys can make them easier to hunt than some ducks, because they are susceptible to good calling.

Photo courtesy of R. L. Davis, Jr.

Goose silhouettes mixed with shells and full body decoys work well for Canada geese.

Goose hunting is usually on fields, so dry-land decoys are the rule. Most hunters believe a minimum of four or five dozen are needed; others use twice that. But some hunters, especially those with stuffed goose decoys, can get by with two or three dozen. Generally the bigger and more realistic your decoys are, the fewer you need.

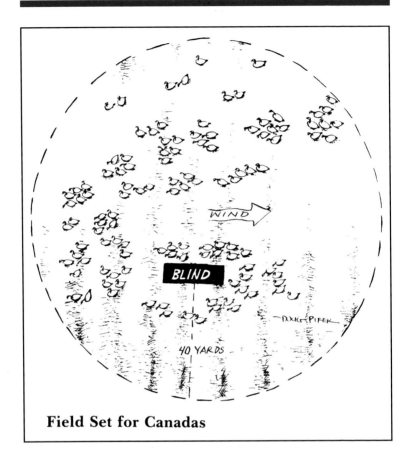

Field Set for Canadas

Geese, like ducks, prefer to land into the wind without flying over fellow waterfowl on the ground. Your spread should accommodate this, with a cup-shaped pattern facing the wind, or two groups with an opening between them. Try to get the geese to come from the front or one side of the blind intending to land just in front of you.

Grounded geese nearly always face the wind, so the majority of your decoys should, too. About two geese for every dozen should be "sentinels," with heads up, with the rest "feeders" or "sleepers." For a touch of realism, arrange the rig in groups of four to eight decoys, representing family units.

Canada goose hunters are divided on whether it is effective to mix types of decoys. Those who do usually combine a silhouette, or plastic type with a big bunch of windsock-style decoys. In a breeze, it appears

Photo courtesy of R. L. Davis, Jr.

Water rigs for Canadas consist of floating blocks set around the blind within gun range, along with some high-ground decoys at water's edge.

Photo courtesy of The Mighty Layout Boys, LLC.

Waterfowl nearly always land into the wind and on a fairly open spot on the water. Knowing this, you can rig your decoys to encourage ducks and geese to attempt landing near your blind.

that some of the "birds" are standing while others are walking. It also helps to put two or three windsocks a little off to the side, simulating a small group that has landed and is walking to join the main flock. These should be in or near your spread's landing pocket.

Canada goose decoys are usually spread about three to five feet apart. Some silhouette rigs have three dekes to a single unit, almost touching. But this is no problem because all three slim forms cannot be seen from the same angle. No edge of the spread should be farther than 45 yards from the blind to ensure decoying birds come into range. Even if you have a well-made landing pocket at close range, birds may try to land at the edge of the pattern.

Field hunters usually use pits or layout blinds well away from any shelter—although fence row blinds can sometimes be effective.

Water rigs for Canada goose hunters are basically the same as puddle duck sets, though at least three dozen goose decoys are recommended. Floating decoys are set out from the shoreline, and some high-ground decoys are set around a small, well-camouflaged blind. Field pits are generally more successful than water blinds when Canadas are resting in large flocks in large bodies of open water. However, a small pond in the center of a cornfield, where you can use both floater and field decoys, can be a very successful set-up.

Decoying Snow Geese

Snow goose hunting is pretty much confined to high ground. Snows are considered by experts to be less wary than Canadas, but their habit of moving by the hundreds makes them hard to decoy. The main secret to decoying snows is to put huge numbers of decoys in the right field at the right time. Some snow goose hunters have success with smaller rigs by luring small groups of geese as they come off their roost before joining with more birds.

Because so many decoys—up to 2,000—are needed, snow goose hunters usually use the lightest and cheapest available. The game is less wary than most, so these decoys don't need to be fancy. Diapers, newspapers, plastic bags, and other white objects about the size of snow geese are commonly used. Some hunters believe that snow geese are wising up to these tricks, however, and that more realistic decoys work better today. If you can afford a complete rig of plastic snow goose shells or windsocks, use them; if you can't, buy a few and fill out the rig with the cheaper decoys.

Photo courtesy R. L. Davis, Jr.

Big spreads of snows and blues may also lure in larger groups of Canada geese.

Snow goose hunters typically find a field the geese are using and return the next morning to spread at least several hundred decoys. The most realistic ones are placed on the downwind side, where hunters lie under white sheets or in white coats that look like the decoys. Snows, like all waterfowl, will often attempt to land on the downwind side. But they are not predictable. When a big flock finally decides to land, the white birds may come milling around and drifting down everywhere— a sight that a waterfowler will never forget.

Photo courtesy R. L. Davis, Jr.

Snow goose rag spreads can be enhanced with manufactured sentinel and feeder heads.

Other Decoys and Rigs

Waterfowlers pursuing the less-hunted species may not be able to find those types of decoys, or they may not be able to justify the expense of a whole new decoy outfit. Often, hunters can get by with other types of decoys that they may already have.

Whistling swans, open game in only a few states, can be attracted with the larger snow goose decoys. As in snow goose hunting, larger rigs are better, and whistling swan hunting may often coincide with snow goose hunting. Swans, experiencing little hunting pressure, are not as wary as most other species. They are characterized by their tendency to fly in small family flocks and approach decoys with a gradual, angled descent.

Brant hunters also have good luck with decoys of other species. Canada goose blocks are most often employed, usually in a combination land/water rig in feeding areas.

Specialty Decoys

Anything a hunter can do to impart realism to his decoy spread enhances his chances to bag birds. Job one is setting realistic decoys in a natural pattern. Blocks on choppy water will have a realistic swimming motion. But if it's calm, hunters have to make the motion.

In the cover of flooded timber, a common practice is for hunters to splash water with their feet. This simulates ducks diving below the surface for feed. The decoys themselves don't have to move — the splashes and rings of waves are enough to convince ducks that dinner is served.

148

Photo courtesy of M. Embrey

The convenience and mobility of stackable shell decoys and silhouettes allows goose hunters to hunt fields seldom hunted.

Your spread can take on a very lifelike appearance with a system that makes a few of the decoys move. For a series of decoys that twist and splash, tie three or four blocks to a line that extends from your blind to a solid object or anchor. As the decoys drift to one side, jerk the rope and pull them back in line. Occasionally tugging the line, especially when game is in sight, will create enticing movement. This rig can be improved by fastening a long spring between the rope and anchor. Heavykeeled decoys that won't tip, and good cover to hide your arm movement, are the keys to this system.

Another apparatus is the tipping decoy, which simulates a feeding puddler. A line is attached to a hole in the decoy's bill, running straight down to a screw eye in a heavy anchor, and back to the hunter's hand. As the hunter pulls, the line slides through the eye and jerks the decoy down headfirst in a natural feeding tip.

A few waterfowlers use a motorized decoy, which "swims" about with a battery-operated propeller. It must be rigged carefully to keep from getting tangled or otherwise put out of commission, but does not require manual operation like the other devices.

149

Flag waving, an attractor that simulates ducks or geese flapping their wings, often gets excellent results for Canadas, snows, and sea ducks.

High-ground hunters use windsocks and kite decoys for the attraction of movement. Flag waving can also fool geese and some ducks into believing that fellow waterfowl are landing or flapping their wings. There are even motorized Canada goose decoys that flap their wings—at the price of a decent duck boat.

CHAPTER 9

CALLS AND CALLING

There is nothing more deadly on a lonesome mallard than a good duck call. On the other hand, poor callers have probably done more for waterfowl conservation than the Migratory Bird Treaty Act.

More than one flock with full intentions of dropping into a decoy spread has been turned away by an unpracticed, tone-deaf, or overanxious caller. Ducks and geese have finely tuned hearing that can distinguish a poor call, even a single off-key note. The wrong sound sets off warning bells that waterfowl immediately heed.

This is not to say you have to sound exactly like a duck or goose to attract them. Some calls sound unlike any call any waterfowl makes, yet they work. You need not be the maestro of the marsh, either. Experts concur you can call ducks with only a couple quacks of their vocabulary.

But these must be very well-done quacks, with the right pitch, cadence, and "texture." To consistently fool waterfowl, you must have a good repertoire of near-perfect imitations, or learn to sound *better* than a real duck.

Getting Started

The procedure for becoming a good waterfowl caller is this: Buy a good call (or more than one) that is popular with successful callers in your area. At the same time, buy tapes or records that teach you the right tone, tempo, and timing for calling various species. Learn some basic calls, then spend time talking to waterfowl to gauge your results. Keep an open mind and try to learn as much as possible from your successes and mistakes.

Field experience may show you that hen mallards and geese—especially snow geese—are the most vocal waterfowl. Since mallards are so talkative and social, swimming with nearly every other species, their calls work for other types of ducks, too.

Duck Calling

There are three schools of thought in calling ducks. The first approach is to call only as an attention-getter, just to let ducks in the neighborhood know where to look for your decoys. This is usually wise advice

151

A good blind location and decoy rig are critical elements in being able to call ducks and geese to the gun.

for the novice caller. He needs to advertise, yet calling conservatively cuts the chances of making the inevitable mistake that changes a duck's mind and sends it winging for the horizon.

The opposite method is to call constantly; the caller blows nonstop for fear that some duck may pass without the privilege of hearing his music. Hunters who advance this system are either the real experts

152

Photo courtesy of R. L. Davis, Jr.

The wide variety of calls on the market can be perplexing to the beginner trying to decide which to buy. Seek some advice—and maybe a lesson or two—from a successful waterfowler in your area.

who never make mistakes, or raw beginners who have no idea what they're doing.

Success somewhere between these extremes is what the caller should strive for. Calling beyond the attention-getter—actually working a bird or flock with a variety of calls—is how the hunter finds joy in calling. There is great satisfaction in knowing when, where, why, and how to use calls, and then using them to call birds to the gun.

Calling varies by species, region, and individual caller. Several calling systems have been developed, each with its own variations. Even

Wary waterfowl often pass several times at the edge of gun range before dropping in or winging out. The dilemma is whether to wait for a surer shot, at the risk of *not getting* a shot. Never pull the trigger until you're sure the bird is well within range.

among the most successful calling systems there are contradictions, and hunters are advised to study, practice, field test, and decide on the method best for them.

There are other factors that affect calling success. Many "expert callers" are hunters who simply have the experience and knack to pick good feeding sites and blind locations. They don't waste effort on "uncallable" birds flying high a quarter mile away. They look for the small bunches or low-flying single giving indications they can be called: altering wingbeats or bobbing their heads around, looking for a place to plant their feet. With experience, it's easy to pick out birds that are hearing and responding to your call from ones with a definite, distant destination.

Operating the Call

Most duck and goose calls are operated in the same manner. Place the top of the barrel, or large end of the call, against your upper lip. In this position, the effect will be to blow through the bottom half of the mouthpiece. Grasp the opposite end of the call in your loosely closed fist, holding the tip between your thumb and forefinger. Thus, you can change tone and project the sound in different directions by opening and closing your fingers.

Start by making a single quack with the call. To accomplish this, grunt the word "quit" or "hoot" into the call, forcing air not with your mouth but with your diaphragm. At the end of the note, your tongue should close quickly to the roof of your mouth to cut the note off sharply. Concentrate on single notes until you have mastered the sound.

To actually call ducks, you must put a series of these quacks together, with changes in tone and cadence, to simulate actual duck language. Most beginning duck callers should practice four types of calls: the hail or highball, greeting call, come-back call, and feeding calls.

Photo courtesy of R. L. Davis, Jr.

To operate a standard waterfowl call, place the end of the barrel against your upper lip with your hand gripping the insert. Force air through the call with your diaphragm, not your mouth or throat, and use your fingers to alternately muffle and funnel the sound.

155

The Hail Call

The hail is the all-important attention-getting call, and probably the most difficult to master. It is the initial sound the duck hunter makes on spotting a distant flock within hearing range.

The hail call consists of forceful, urgent, or pleading sounds that say, "I'm over here—pay attention to me!" The call is a series of about 10-20 very loud, high, even-pitch notes, followed by a series descending in pitch and volume. The secret to a good hail call is to make all of the first notes identical in tone: loud, clear, confident, and sassy. As you descend the scale, make sure every note is lower than the last. For maximum effect, direct the sound right at the ducks.

Photo courtesy of R. L. Davis, Jr.

Try a variety of waterfowl call designs to see which gets the best results for you.

(The following diagrams indicate the tone and tempo in making various duck calls. The X signifies a brief note and the 0 stands for a note of longer duration. The bars, like a musical scale, indicate higher notes at the top and lower ones at the bottom.)

Hail Call

X	X	X	X	X	X	X	X
						X	
							X
							X

Often, only once or twice with the hail series is all that's necessary to turn a flock and get them homed-in on your decoys.

Most expert callers blow the hail series twice and then wait to see the flock's reaction. Ducks may respond in many ways, such as turning their heads in flight, slowly banking around, or subtlely changing their wing beat. Learn to read their body language.

Photo courtesy of R. L. Davis, Jr.

The calling necessary to toll ducks to the gun varies depending on the situation. At times, a single hail series will get the job done; other times, ducks need careful coaxing.

Under some conditions, expert callers can bring in ducks and geese without the help of a decoy spread. Birds home-in on the sound.

When a flock fails to respond to your hail call, repeat the series several times, speeding it up and sounding more excited.

If you can turn a flock with your hail series, it may be the only call you need—the decoys may do the rest. In fact, inexperienced callers are usually best off if they do *not* call as long as ducks are headed their way. More calling only increases the chances of making a mistake and turning the ducks away.

More experienced callers, however, use the greeting call as soon as ducks turn toward them. The greeting is a natural call, sounding more like a real hen mallard, that welcomes ducks to join the decoys.

The Greeting Call

The greeting call has some similarity to the hail, but usually with less volume, accomplished by partly closing the end of the call with your fingers. The greeting call contains all descending notes (about five to ten) and shorter series:

Greeting Call

X X	X	O	
X X	X	X	
X X	X	X	
X X	X		
X X	X		

As indicated, the greeting call is blown in different types of series. In the first series, tones descend the scale slowly. In the second series, there is more of a drop in pitch between each note. The third series has a prolonged initial note, followed by a quickly dropping series. These three series may be blown in any sequence.

If the birds have your rig pinpointed, try to throw the call out over your decoys so it seems the call is coming from them.

The Come-Back Call

If the flock turns away from either your hail or greeting call, you may be able to bring them back with the more intense come-back call. It has an excited or pleading sound, with louder, faster notes. Remember to keep the notes clear and crisp with air pushed from your diaphragm and turned off and on with your tongue and upper throat.

Come-Back Call

```
   X              O
     X            X
      X             X
        X             X
          X             X
           X              X
```

Never in any of these calls should you begin with lower tones and slide up the scale, then back down. This is among the beginner's most common mistakes. Always start high and end low—calls that raise in pitch or burst out in apparent surprise are alarm calls that will chase ducks away.

Wrong Way

```
      X
    X   X
  X       X
            X
            X
```

If a flock comes flying very near or directly overhead but out of range, you may blow calls sounding like contented ducks sitting on the

water. These include the feeding chuckle, the lonesome hen, and the
contented mallard calls. They may be blown together in a series.

Photo courtesy of R. L. Davis, Jr.

**Keep a sharp eye on waterfowl you are working with the call. Their be-
havior dictates the pattern of sounds you should make.**

The Feeding Calls

The feeding chuckle may be difficult to master right away. It is made by
blowing the sound "kitty" or "tukka" in a duck call, and sounds similar
to growling or gargling. The chuckle is very rapid. Flick your tongue
rapidly up and down to make this call. If you have a hard time making
the call, start slowly and speed up gradually. It is also a good idea to slip
in an occasional quack or two when running the chuckle. The lonesome
hen call is a drawnout call of three notes. The contented mallard call,
often heard among flocks just before sunrise and during feeding, is also
three notes. The first is drawn-out and higher pitched, followed by two
shorter notes descending in pitch.

To simulate the chatter of several ducks feeding, two or more hunters
may call at the same time, making the same or different calls. Multiple
callers can be very effective provided they are proficient. Teaching your
partner how to blow a duck call should not be done in a hunting situation; nor is that a place to practice.

Feeding Calls

O

X

KITTY-KITTY   O O O

Calling Other Ducks

Because puddle ducks intermingle freely, other species will respond to mallard calls. Black ducks, pintails, teal, wigeon, and wood ducks can

Photo courtesy of R. L. Davis, Jr.

Splashing water in flooded timber adds sight and sound effects to your calling and decoying efforts, simulating the commotion of feeding ducks.

all be lured by the sound of a hen mallard. High-pitched mallard calls are the standard for luring gadwall and shovelers. There are also specialized calls for the other species.

Most western and some eastern pintail hunters use whistle calls for these ducks, though mallard quacks are commonly used. Conversely, call-shy mallards can be fooled by pintail whistles.

In operating a pintail call, "gargle" as you blow to create a sound similar to a police whistle. Wigeon and green-winged teal are called with the same or similar whistles—single notes for teal and varying series for wigeon. Blue-winged teal sound like a very high-pitched mallard; blow the word "tick" into a blue-wing call to make the right sound. Wood ducks are called with shrill notes made by saying the word "wheat" into a wood duck call. When they are heading in your direction, choke down on the call and make it squeal like a high-pitched whistle.

The peeps and tirrs from these calls are usually for confidence after the ducks have spotted your decoys.

Diving ducks can be called quite readily on a standard duck call. The call is made by trilling your tongue in the mouthpiece, making a medium-pitched, gutteral "brrrrr, brt" sound. The call should be quicker for scaup, slower and coarser for redheads and canvasbacks. As a rule, calls are progressively lower-pitched as the size of the diver increases.

Goose Calling

Goose calls are somewhat easier to master than duck calls, because proper form and a few variances in air pressure are all that's necessary to make the right sounds.

Like blowing a duck call, you can operate a goose call by "grunting" air up with your diaphragm. Goose calls require controlling the air with your throat, mouth, and tongue, along with muffling the end of the tube with your hand.

Types of Goose Calls

The Canada is by far the most sought-after goose. To call the Canada, you have to make hail honks, clucks, feeding gabble, and other sounds.

The first call to learn is the hail—a simple series of honks. Some experts believe only the high note of the common Canada honk is necessary, but most callers start with a low growl sound that quickly jumps to the high-pitched note.

To make the two-note call, bring air up from your diaphragm and say the word "what" into the call. The "wh" part makes the low sound as the caller blows a moderate amount of air through the call. The sound leaps up the scale, hitting a high pitch with a sudden increase in air, and is stopped with the "at" part of the call. The hail call usually starts at a leisurely pace, progressing to a fast, nonstop series of these honks.

The cluck is an important call that holds the attention of geese that are coming your way. The cluck is a greatly abbreviated form of the two-note honk. It includes both high and low notes, intermingled sporadically, and should be presented with an excited, rapid-fire delivery. While the hail call is often best delivered by a single caller, several callers are better to make the cluck call sound natural.

Photo courtesy R. L. Davis, Jr.

Canada geese are fairly susceptible to good calling if it is accompanied by a realistic decoy spread.

A third call for Canadas, the feeding gabble, is similar in function to the mallard feeding chuckle. It is made with short grunts, or by saying the words "ha-ha-ha-ha..." into the call. It takes a lot of practice to be able to blow a fast series for moderate durations between breaths.

Another Canada call is similar to the contented mallard quack. It is a short, high-pitched honk with lower volume than a hail call. This call is made with short bursts of breath, or by saying the word "hut" repeatedly into the call.

Sequence of Calls

In a typical hunting situation, hunters spot geese from the blind and give the hail call. Sky-high flocks in V formation seldom respond to the call, but lower, smaller groups of geese often will. Geese looking for a place to land can often be lured from a quarter-mile or more, depending on conditions.

163

Keep calling while the geese are in sight. If they turn toward you, start giving fast clucks. If hunting a field, you may switch to the feeding gabble and contented honks when geese are about 100 yards away. Continue calling until it is time to shoot. If the geese pass out of range or turn away, an excited, pleading hail may bring them back.

Photo courtesy R. L. Davis, Jr.

Hunters rigged out for both snows and Canadas make as much commotion as they can with their calls. They have to sound like a real squabbling flock and compete with the live birds.

Calling Snow Geese

Calling snow geese is similar to calling Canadas, though the snow goose call is much higher-pitched without the pronounced low moaning sound. Snow goose calls sound like fast, high-pitched barking of dogs. Blowing the word "tut" into the call gives this sound.

Hunters usually use a very fast tempo, with several hunters calling at once, to attract snow goose flocks. There is also a gabble feeding call (a low-end murmur) and contented honk similar to the Canada goose calls. Make this by blowing "ho-ho-ho-ho." The difference is that the snow goose is noisier, higher, and faster. With snow geese, the more racket you make, the better.

Calling White-Fronted Geese

The white-fronted goose, or specklebelly, has a unique call different from Canadas or snows. The speck's chuckling call lends another name to the white-front: laughing goose.

Among the speck's many calls is the two-note yodel, made by saying "wa-wa-wa-wa..." into the call. Both high-pitched and low-pitched yodels are used for the hail call. The specklebelly feeding call is made by grunting "kuluck" into the tube.

Start with the hail call when you spot a far-off flock. The objective is to give two yodels, and hopefully get one in response. When the geese yodel three times in succession, it means they are suspicious. If they stop responding, ignore it and continue with your cadence.

When the flock gets close, switch to the feeding call and continue calling until the moment you shoot.

Photo courtesy of R.L. Davis, Jr.

Mastering different types of calls can pay big dividends in the field.

The Secret of Waterfowl Calling

No matter which species you wish to call, there is an audio or video tape on the market to teach you proper calling. All beginning and intermediate callers are advised to obtain and study these instructional aids. To be a successful caller, you should study the art extensively and practice as much as you can in the off season. Only with experience will you be able to "read" the ducks and learn what subtle variation in pitch, tone, volume, and note duration will pull in the ducks when other callers can't.

Photo courtesy R. L. Davis, Jr.

CHAPTER 10

SPECIAL WATERFOWLING TECHNIQUES

T here are times when hunting big waters and sprawling marshes simply doesn't work, when massive decoy spreads and the most expert calling can't attract birds. Sometimes this is because calm, bluebird weather leaves ducks content and inactive. Other times it's because heavy hunting pressure makes ducks exceedingly wary of spreads and calls. Under such conditions, sitting in a blind is boring and unproductive.

But if the ducks don't come to you, you can go to the ducks. Jump shooting, potholing, sneak boating, or float hunting—these aggressive kinds of duck hunting produce when decoying and calling fail. Special tactics are also needed to hunt swans and wary big-water birds.

Jump Shooting

Most jump shooting and potholing pivots on puddle ducks. The most widely encountered species in jump shooting are mallards, black ducks, wood ducks, pintails, and the teals. However, all the nondiving species can be found, depending on the region. And when rough weather hammers the big waters, some of the divers like bluebills, canvasbacks, and goldeneyes will venture into streams and inland ponds.

In many respects, jump shooting and potholing can be more like upland hunting than big-water duck hunting. The hunter is constantly on the move, stalking potholes, following creeks or irrigation ditches, checking out stubble fields, and visiting big puddles that occur in hardwoods or agricultural fields after heavy or constant rains. Migrating ducks will drop in practically anywhere that promises security and food. Likewise, when there is heavy hunting pressure, the birds will use very small waters that are seldom, if ever, hunted.

Photos courtesy of M. Fleming

Jumpshooting small potholes and creeks provides fast action without the work of other types of waterfowling. It is often combined with upland hunting.

Jump shooting blends the stalking tactics of big game hunting with the constant movement of upland bird hunting. It means following creeks and streams quietly, utilizing the bank cover to remain unseen. You may have to hunch low or even crawl. Birds on small waters or stubble fields are always alert, and they'll flush quickly at a hint of danger. A prerequisite for successful jump shooting is patience; move slowly, always trying to keep low and blend into the cover.

One can expect species to differ in their selection of small waters. Wood ducks can be quite widespread. They'll use farmland ponds, ditches, and standing water. Oak groves can provide excellent sport, for wood ducks like to feed on fallen acorns. After a rainy spell, prowl the oaks in hilly country and expect woodies to be in the temporary puddles standing at the bases of hills.

Mallards also use woodland ponds, but prefer more open places such as marsh-rimmed ditches and ponds. If they pitch into timber, it'll mainly be tall flooded hardwoods. In general, mallards and blacks like more sizeable waters than woodies use; the wood duck will land on a

Photos courtesy of M. Fleming

A good duck stalker can sneak up on a flock of mallards in flooded timber. In thick stuff, he must be a good snap shooter, too.

bathtub-size spot, whereas mallards and blacks like more room to ma-neuver. However, mallards and black ducks are found on moving water more often than woodies. Trout streams and other relatively shallow creeks and rivers host mallards and blacks, along with some teal. None of these species enjoys fighting the current; they can be expected on back eddies and other slack water as well as behind brushy shoreline obstructions that break the flow and offer food.

Pintails tend to follow mallards and blacks in their selections. Teal can be widely distributed, but the best spots seem to be ponds and slow-moving water in the more open areas where they can use their straight-away speed instead of having to fight their way through cover.

169

Photo courtesy of Wayne Gendron

Geese may be taken by jumpshooting, but it takes planning, a knowledge of the area, and a stealthy stalk.

When jump shooting moving water, try to scout the flow before opening day. Remember where the most-likely resting and feeding spots are and get to them as silently as possible. Merely following a bank can work, but it's not as effective as planning ahead and sneaking up on the prime sites. Wear camo so you don't spook birds from a distance, and don't be a slave to the course of the waterway. At some points, such as a hairpin turn, it may be wise to cross the stream and cut across the land to reach a more favorable location. In other words, jump shooting means planning ahead and stalking certain locations rather than simply walking the bank and hoping for something to happen.

When hunting waterfowl on foot near deep water, you need a plan to retrieve downed birds. A dog, net, or fishing pole with gang hooks on a floating plug are great aids. If you can't retrieve it, don't shoot it.

Floating back-country waterways in a canoe is a good way to sneak up on elusive puddlers. It can provide day-long action when birds aren't out flying.

Float Hunting

On wider, navigable streams, and where local laws permit, a waterfowl-hunting float trip can be action packed. Done correctly, floating can get you closer to more ducks than walking.

Two of the more important rules in float hunting are: (1) Always cut to the inside of corners to get closer to ducks around the bend. Swinging wide lets ducks see you sooner at longer range. (2) Be alert to dangers of shooting from a boat and let the bow person be the sole shooter. It is dangerous for the stern man to shoot or even handle a shotgun.

Most important in float hunting is to keep from betraying your presence. Don't bump around in the boat or let it bounce off rocks. Try to keep from making ripples that can give advance notice of your arrival.

The most successful float hunters keep themselves and their boats camouflaged. A miniature blind or camouflage screen at the bow hides occupants and gives the boat an appearance of floating debris. The front screen should be high enough to totally conceal the crouching front shooter, and is best if it is large enough to hide the movements of the man guiding the boat. It should not be unnecessarily large, however. The shooter should be able to see and shoot over it by sitting erect.

The bow blind may be made of evergreen boughs, burlap, or one of the commercial camo covers or blinds. It should have a small porthole or two for the shooter to look through.

For solitary hunters, the innertube belly boat commonly used for bass fishing can be a very effective float-hunting vehicle. With good camouflage clothing and maybe a small branch or two, this rig can closely resemble floating debris. With a pair of swim fins, it can be the most maneuverable craft and let the hunter penetrate the smallest and most jungly waters.

A trick used by many float hunters is to set some decoys at an easily accessible area (or several) that they plan to float through. These sets may attract ducks that would have otherwise passed by, providing more shooting opportunities. The decoys should be set at an optimum shooting site, such as just downstream on the inside of a sharp curve.

Like the land-bound jump shooters, float hunters can expect a variety of shooting situations. Most will be flushing-game shots, but there will be many crossing shots and the difficult overhead passing shots at birds flying from ahead or behind.

Guns for jump shooting need the high energy of waterfowl guns but the handling ease of upland guns. Barrels of 21 to 26 inches are best for most shooters. The long waterfowl barrels can be too sluggish for fast-flushing birds.

The 12-gauge is tops among jump-shooting guns, especially if it has a three-inch chamber. For lead shot, a full-choke barrel and No. 5 or No. 4 shot is a sound all-around combination. If the gun is a double, the first barrel could well be a modified choke with No. 5 shot for the first close-in chance with the other a full choke with 4s. If birds are skittish and longer flushes are common, magnum loads of No. 2 shot are fine if they hold a tight pattern for multiple hits.

Heavy pellets and dense patterns are desirable for jump shooting, because the birds are often outgoing targets and optimum pellet energy is needed to drive through heavy down and reach vital areas. With lead shot, buffered magnum and copper-plated pellets are state-of-the-art for anchoring jumped ducks.

With steel, changes are necessary. Steel No. 4s are marginal for 35 to 45 yard work on heavily-downed ducks. Steel No. 1s or 2s are recommended as a universal choice to bridge the distance and arrive

Photo courtesy of M. Embrey

Diligent scouting and being creative can get you to areas seldom hunted.

with adequate per-pellet energy. As stated in Chapter 5, however, steel No. 1s may pattern better from a modified or improved-modified choke than from a full choke; hence, some test patterning is suggested to determine optimum efficiency.

A pair of binoculars helps considerably in jump shooting by letting the hunter spot distant birds so he can plan his stalk. Camouflaged clothes and some practice on trapshooting or skeet will also help you get on target faster and more accurately.

Thus, if the ducks don't come to you, you can go to them. Whether you stalk ponds or streams, put some decoys on a small farmland pothole, or float the river in a canoe, it works when all else fails. And in many cases, you'll have much less hunting pressure to contend with.

Pass Shooting

Another popular form of waterfowl hunting, especially for Canada geese, is pass shooting around refuge perimeters. It isn't classic hunting, but for many people without access to private farmland, it may be the only available way to hunt geese. In all honesty, such refuge line hunting is mainly shooting, not hunting, and the main concern is for optimum equipment rather than decoying and/or calling techniques. The hunters rely on the birds' morning and afternoon departures for this action. Finding where birds leave and enter the refuge at low altitude, keeping well-hidden, and picking your shots, are the keys to successful pass shooting.

Too often, refuge line pass shooting results in the practice of sky-busting, which is the reckless, long-distance shooting at birds out of shotgun range. It does nothing but illustrate the poor judgment and lack of knowledge about shotshell performance of many hunters. Moreover,

Photo courtesy of M. Fleming

Pass shooting is legitimate sport if a hunter avoids the refuge-line mob scene and resists the temptation of skybusting out-of-range flocks.

the crowded conditions along refuge lines often spark unsportsmanlike incidents that we could do without. But approached with knowledge and responsibility, pass shooting from well-located blinds can be productive, enjoyable, and legitimate sport.

Geese are big birds, and they are deceptive targets; they can appear huge even though they are at marginal range or beyond. To be a good judge of range, one should spend time afield practicing to judge distance. With the tremendous expansion of Canada geese, most hunters have the chance to study range estimation, as well as calls and behavior, with semiwild birds at parks, golf course ponds, etc. As a rough gauge, a 12-bore shotgun's muzzle will cover a Canada's body and much of its wings at 50 yards. When a 12-gauge's muzzle blots out the entire bird, or several birds in a flock, they are out of range.

Layout, Sculling, and Sneak Boats

Layout Gunning

A thrilling way to hunt diving ducks and Canadas is layout gunning. This requires specialized boats and several hunters, and is usually confined to large bodies of water. In the middle of the decoy spread, a low-profile layout boat is anchored. The sides of the boat slope down to the water's edge. The gunner lies on his back, hidden behind the sides of the boat, with only the top of his head lifted above the gunwales. Waterfowl approach the decoys unaware of the small, low-sided boat hidden in the midst of the rig. When the birds are within range, the gunner rises, picks his target, and shoots from a sitting position. This may prove very challenging for the hunter depending on the size of the waves and the speed of the wind. Once a bird has been downed, the gunner uses colored flags to signal a tender boat that he has a dead bird or a cripple to be retrieved. The hunting party takes turns manning the tender boat or gunning from the layout boat. The tender boat, standing by in case of emergency, is also used to transport hunters, decoys, and the layout boat to the gunning site.

While this method of hunting is very effective, it may also be dangerous for inexperienced people in rough weather. There are guides who offer layout boat hunting, and a day with one of them is advised before getting into layout gunning on your own. There are commercial layout boats made of wood and canvas or fiberglass.

Photo courtesy of Mighty Layout Boys, LLC.

Layout gunning is a thrilling and effective way to take ducks and geese that are shy of shoreline blinds.

Sneakboat Gunning

Similar to layout hunting is stalking with the mobile sneakboat. Using a sneakboat to quietly approach resting or feeding ducks removes any threat that a blind may present to the birds. Decoys are placed in a wide open stretch of the river or lake. Since there is no land or foreign object within several hundred yards, the divers or puddle ducks readily pitch into your decoys. Hunters watch from a blind on the shore or an island upriver from the rig, glassing the decoys until a flock lands. With the birds in and around the decoys, the hunter quietly launches the sneak-

Photo courtesy of Mighty Layout Boys, LLC.

Layout gunners after big-water divers experience the thrills of fast shooting and precariously small boats.

boat. Boats resemble a flat-topped canoe with a canvas blind extending up one side. This blind is on a collapsible frame that tapers down to both bow and stern. Both one- and two-man models are used. Often a small outboard is hung on a side motor mount to speed up the boat's return to the blind. The boat is propelled with small hand paddles and steering is by a T-shaped bar in the front of the boat. This bar is attached to cables running to the rear of the boat and controlling a long rudder. Even though the ducks may see you, the decoys hold them from flight. A quiet, steady approach will get you within range. The blind is dropped and as the birds jump, you are ready to shoot. (Don't forget to check local/state regulations to see if sneakboats are legal in your area.)

Sculling Boat Gunning

Similar in effect to sneakboats are sculling boats. A sculling boat is long, usually two-man, with a square stern and a pointed bow. A hole in the upper half of the stern has a long oar extending down through it into the water. The front man is the gunner. He patiently lies against his backrest and keeps an eye on the birds being approached. The rear man, also lying, holds the oar over his shoulder and moves it in a figure-8 motion. The boat is propelled silently. As with the sneakboat, the birds hopefully will take no notice or at least be unalarmed by the low-profile boat's approach. Either of these two boats may be used without decoys on a float trip.

Swan Hunting

In a few areas of the country, especially in the West, hunters pursue the largest and most elegant of huntable waterfowl: the tundra swan.

The tundra, or whistling, swan has been hunted in Utah, California, and other western states for about 20 years, and recently the first Atlantic flyway hunting was opened in North Carolina, due to increasing swan populations. All states that allow swan hunting have limited permits.

Most swan hunting is pass shooting near refuges along borders and on dikes extending into the water. Swans can also be decoyed on water or in fields with moderately large spreads of large snow goose decoys.

Averaging 15 pounds, swans are considerably larger than Canada geese. Big bores, heavy loads, and large pellet sizes are a must for hunting swans.

These birds are excellent eating, particularly the younger swans.

Coot Hunting

The true coot, considered a "junk duck" by many waterfowlers, is actually a member of the rail family. These slate-black birds, also called mudhens, are familiar sights in shallow backwaters as they half fly, half run across the surface of the water ahead of duck boats.

The coot's lobed rather than webbed feet and its rather sluggish nature restrict its take-off and flying ability. This, combined with its passive attitude from lack of hunting, makes it a fairly easy target for those who do hunt coot.

Photo courtesy of Lonnie Coates

Photo courtesy of M. Embrey

Sneakboating employs a small, camouflaged boat to float up on an open-water decoy rig after ducks or geese have landed there. It is an advanced method of waterfowl hunting, both exciting and productive.

Tundra swans, hunted in only a few areas of the U.S., may be the water-fowler's ultimate trophy.

Coots are usually hunted from a shallow-draft boat rowed or poled slowly through marsh. Coot hunting, with its ample action, is a good primer for beginning waterfowlers. Because coots fly very close to the water, the shooter can see where his shots are hitting by the splash his pellets make.

While it is edible, the mudhen's appetite for unsavory sustenance has given him a reputation as poor tablefare. A well-known recipe for coot is to place a brick in the body cavity, roast at 400 degrees until the brick turns soft, and then throwaway the coot and eat the brick!

Paying to Hunt

A scarcity of time and places to hunt have prompted many waterfowlers to hire guides and lease hunting lands. The best approach when taking this route is to shop around and know what you're getting.

If you only get to hunt waterfowl a few times of year, don't have time to scout or handle equipment, and want a good hunt, a guided trip may be the way to go. Get reliable references and talk with several guides before making a selection. When you hire a guide, make sure you both understand what he is to provide, what your duties will be, and how much it will cost. You may want to draft a simple contract.

Hunting leases are more popular each year as more hunters crowd public lands and permission to hunt private property is harder to obtain. Leases are of the most advantage to hunters in clubs who want to hunt frequently in the same area. The better leased hunting properties often offer the best hunting in the area. But some clubs have been disappointed by poor success. Before you lease, talk with the party who previously leased the land, if possible. Scout the property thoroughly and maybe rent it for one season before entering into a long-term lease. Make sure you and the landowner both understand each other's obligations, such as installation of blinds and times of activity. If you lease an active farm, the dates and methods of crop harvest and water diversion will be critical to your success.

Part IV

The Complete Waterfowler

Photo courtesy of R. L. Davis, Jr.

Photo courtesy of R. L. Davis, Jr.

CHAPTER 11

SHOTGUNS, WATER, AND SAFETY

E very year, waterfowl hunters suffer serious and unnecessary accidents. This dark truth is not something we want to think about while pursuing our beloved sport. But the danger can't be denied, and it must be on our minds if we want to improve the safety of waterfowling. Poor planning or a seemingly minor lapse in attention can have tragic consequences.

The combination of loaded shotguns, hunters in close proximity, unstable boats, remote hunting sites, dogs, and other factors can create a dangerous situation for waterfowlers. To optimize safety, waterfowl hunters must be aware of the dangers, keep them in mind afield, and take all precautions.

Firearms Safety in Waterfowling

All standard firearms safety rules apply to waterfowling, and the special conditions of duck and goose hunting create more considerations.

While hunting with companions, establish zones of fire, with each hunter shooting only within his assigned area. On float-hunting trips, with both hunters facing downstream, only the forward hunter should be allowed to shoot, with the stern man guiding and stabilizing the boat.

Unload, open the action, and case all shotguns as they are placed into a boat. While hunting, keep the shotgun in each end of the boat pointing out that end, away from all persons on board. Don't shoot unless the boat is stable and secured, and never stand to shoot from a small boat. When transferring guns from a boat to shore or a blind, make sure they are unloaded and the actions are open.

These rules for safety in handling and shooting firearms apply to all situations:

1. Always have control of the gun's muzzle and keep it pointed in a safe direction.

A common cause of serious shotgun accidents is the hunter handling a gun with the muzzle pointed toward himself or others. This usually occurs when transferring shotguns from cars, trucks, boats, and blinds.

2. Be positive of your target's identity before shooting.
3. Be prepared and take time to fire a safe shot. If unsure, or if you must rush so you cannot mount the gun correctly, pass up the shot. If there is any doubt whether you should shoot—don't.
4. Use the right ammunition for your firearm. Carry only one type of ammo to ensure you don't mix different types. A 20-gauge shell loaded into a 12-gauge will slide down the barrel and lodge there. If a 12-gauge shell is loaded behind it and fired, the results can be disastrous.

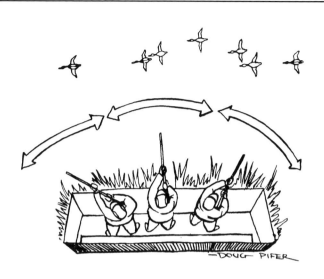

Whatever the situation, always establish zones of fire when hunting with companions. Each hunter should have his own assigned shooting area and never point his gun outside of that area.

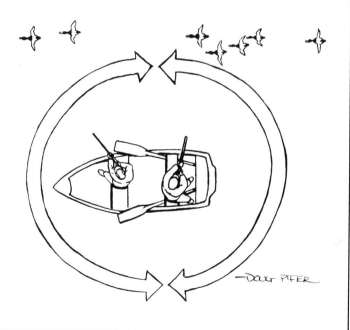

Photo courtesy of R. L. Davis, Jr.

Hunters should use extra caution when standing and shooting in soft, muddy areas.

5. If you fall—and chances are good in a marsh—control the firearm's muzzle. After a fall, unload and check for dirt and damage and make sure the barrel is free of obstructions. If you accidentally dip your shotgun barrel in very cold water, it could cause an ice build-up at the muzzle.

6. Unload your gun before getting into or out of a blind or boat, attempting to climb a steep bank, or traveling across hazardous terrain.

7. When you are alone and must cross a fence, unload your firearm and place it under the fence with the muzzle pointed away from

Boats and blinds around water can require extra safety measures. Hunters should establish shooting zones and use them. Always keep firearm unloaded and stored safely while traveling in a boat.

yourself. When hunting with others and you must cross a fence or similar obstacle, unload the gun and keep the action open. Have one of your companions hold the gun while you cross. Then take their unloaded guns so your companions may cross safely.

8. Maintain your firearm, keep it clean, and never use a gun that is in poor condition, malfunctioning, or incapable of handling the ammunition you use. In cold weather, remove oil and grease from the gun so it cannot congeal and inhibit the action.

9. Be aware of the range of your pellets. Larger goose loads can travel several hundred yards. Make certain your pellets cannot rain down on other hunters, and remember that shotgun pellets can ricochet off water.

10. Adverse conditions and excitement can impair your mental and physical performance. Bulky clothing, rain, wind, snow, etc. can cause poor gun handling and reduce your concentration on safety. Fatigue can cause carelessness and clumsiness, as can the excitement of birds coming in. For maximum safety, control these conditions as much as possible.

11. Be conscious of switching your gun's safety off, and remember to place it back on after the shooting opportunity has passed.

12. Establish zones of fire when hunting next to companions. Be sure your gun's muzzle is *always* pointing into your zone.

13. Alcohol, drugs, and hunting don't mix. Drugs and alcohol may impair your judgment; keen judgment is essential to safe hunting.

14. When you have finished hunting, unload your gun immediately and keep the action open.

15. If companions violate a rule of safe gun handling, refuse to hunt with them unless they correct their behavior.

No firearms safety rule ever prevented an accident. Gun accidents are prevented when people who are handling firearms care enough to do it safely.

Water Safety

If you should fall out of a boat or it should capsize, the cold water and your heavy hunting clothes could cause hypothermia (loss of body heat) or drowning. Most water accidents are preventable when these safety precautions are used:

1. Don't overload the boat or load it off-balance, which could cause the craft to swamp or tip. Heavy gear, hunters, and dogs may make this difficult.

2. Never stand in a boat unless it is solidly secured and your balance is sure. If you stand in an open boat to shoot at waterfowl overhead, the act of looking up or absorbing the gun's recoil could easily throw you off balance and into the water.

3. Make sure your boating equipment is matched and functioning properly. A motor too big for the boat could cause it to swamp; a motor too small for the load could leave you stranded. If your motor fails, you are at the mercy of the elements. Carry oars, a paddle, or some other backup means of propulsion.

4. Be familiar with topography, weather conditions, and equipment before you embark. Know the weather forecast for the day. Know what you're doing before venturing onto big water or a large, maze-like marsh (a compass may help). Know exactly how your boating and safety equipment work, and be able to make small field repairs.

5. Make sure there are personal flotation devices for everyone, that they are in good condition, and that all persons can reach one and

Photo courtesy of R. L. Davis, Jr.

Waterfowlers must be careful wading in water with a soft or slippery bottom, especially when there is a higher risk of drowning or hypothermia.

put it on. Personal flotation devices (PFDs) should be worn as much as possible. A CO_2-inflatable vest or buoyant camouflaged coat will not interfere with hunting.

6. Be aware of the changing weather, daylight, and tides and how they can affect your safety and ability to return. A sudden storm on the water is one of the biggest dangers waterfowlers face.

7. Plan for emergencies and carry the proper equipment. Make sure someone knows where you are going. Along with PFDs and oars, you should have a bailing bucket, tow rope, signaling device, small repair kit, fire-building materials, and other emergency items for special circumstances.

8. Use extreme caution when you walk or wade where your footing is unsure. Algae-covered rocks or submerged trees may make you fall; mud and quagmire may get you stuck. Ice is particularly dangerous—usually thin during waterfowl season. Safe-looking ice can be treacherous.

Photo courtesy of R. L. Davis, Jr.

The combination of wind, wet, cold, and fatigue poses a threat of hypothermia to cold-weather waterfowlers. In some cases, hypothermia can occur in mild weather if the other factors are present.

9. Never travel at night without ample lighting. Darkness can cause you to hit an obstruction and capsize, then prevent you from reaching safety.

10. Never mix boating with alcohol or drugs. Alcohol not only affects your orientation, increasing the chances for an accident, but also lowers your resistance to hypothermia.

Common sense and caution will prevent the great majority of boating accidents, but sometimes mishaps are unavoidable. Wearing a PFD at all times will protect you in an accident against drowning and hypothermia.

Photo courtesy of R. L. Davis, Jr.

Proper clothing helps prevent not only hypothermia, but the fatigue that can lead to accidents.

193

Drowning

Drowning is the second most common cause of accidental death in the U.S. Swimming ability is not a reliable prevention for drowning—many drowning victims are excellent swimmers. Aside from preventing accidents and wearing a PFD, the best ways to avoid drowning are to stay with a capsized boat in most cases, conserve energy if you have to swim or tread water, and try to trap air in hip boots or waders if you have them. Try to signal people on shore or in other boats.

Hypothermia

As dangerous as drowning for the waterfowler is hypothermia. If you are immersed, hypothermia can kill you or cause you to drown in minutes, depending on water temperature. Even out of the water, heat loss from wet, cold, wind, and inappropriate dress can be a serious threat to waterfowl hunters.

A PFD will help a person immersed in cold water conserve body heat, as will waders and clothes. Another way to conserve heat is to pull your knees up to your chest, provided it does not hamper your floating ability. If several persons are in the water, they should conserve body heat by huddling together. The important thing is to get as much of your body out of the water as quickly as possible.

Hypothermia on dry land is a slow, silent killer. It can happen in temperatures as warm as 60 degrees through a combination of wet, wind, and fatigue. Hypothermia victims go through stages beginning with shivering and progressing to loss of muscular control, mental confusion, and unconsciousness. Persons seriously suffering from hypothermia have very pale skin, rigid muscles, and usually are unable to speak.

The only cure for hypothermia is to get the victim warm as quickly as possible. There are, however, many means of prevention. Wear clothes that offer good protection in wind and wet, such as rainsuits or nylon-shell jackets and wool sweaters. Dress in layers. If you think there may be a good chance of getting wet, you may be able to bring a change of dry clothes in a waterproof bag. Don't overexert yourself, as fatigue lowers resistance to cold. Take precautions from getting wet. Carry sources of heat, such as warm drinks in thermos bottles, fire-building material, or Sterno stoves, etc. Common sense is the best prevention.

CHAPTER 12

GAME CARE AND COOKING

Proper care of waterfowl means the difference between delicious and disappointing meals later. Good care begins in the field and the same basic rules apply to all game: keep it clean, cool, and dry. Waterfowl should be bled, opened, and cleaned quickly. Whether or not to "hang" the birds for extended periods is often debated. Some people find it preferable to refrigerate the cleaned birds for no more than a day or two, while others believe waterfowl reaches its peak flavor after aging in the refrigerator for a week or 10 days.

Plucking waterfowl is necessary work and can be done dry, wet, or by a picking machine. Some of the birds are simply skinned. Afterward, the birds should be washed inside and out with cold water, then well dried. Try to remove all shotgun pellets from the carcass; it is not pleasant to bite down on a pellet, especially steel.

To freeze the birds for later use, double wrap them in plastic bags or freezer paper, sealing each package well. Some hunters have good success freezing waterfowl in milk cartons or similar containers. Just fill the container with water, covering the meat. Freezing in water helps prevent freezer burn. Most people find that waterfowl—as well as other kinds of game—are considerably less delectable after freezing. Others believe that freezing reduces gaminess, improving flavor.

Cooking wild ducks and geese is somewhat different from cooking domestic waterfowl since wild birds are usually less tender and less fatty. Age is probably the main determining factor in cooking, so it is important to learn how to determine the age of the birds. Some geese can live to be quite old and will be very tough. In all waterfowl, the legs are the toughest parts.

If you have an old bird, use moist cooking methods such as oven cooking bags, crock pots, pressure cookers, or Dutch ovens. Other ways to help tenderize waterfowl include using wine in marinades and in cooking, soaking the birds in marinade overnight, and steaming or parboiling them before roasting.

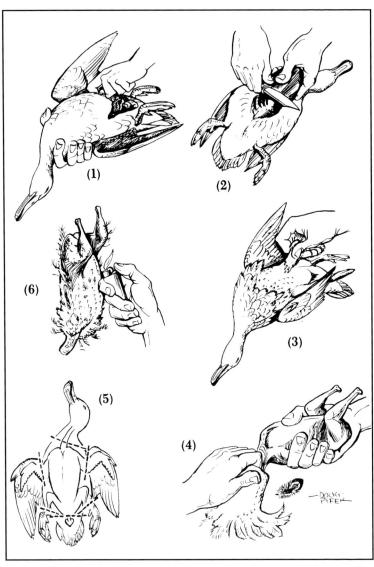

Proper handling of bagged waterfowl saves time and ensures best-quality meat. 1) Most hunters field dress waterfowl soon after shooting, though some leave the entrails in for a couple of days of aging in cool air. 2) Fish-eating ducks can be quite palatable if you remove and cool the breast immediately, and let it marinate before cooking. 3) When dry-plucking waterfowl, pull feathers straight out, just a few at a time, or you may tear the skin. 4) Skinning ducks is much faster than plucking, but you lose the flavorful skin. 5) Remove inedible parts. 6) Singe off the hard-to-pluck pinfeathers.

Many people prefer ducks and geese cooked so the breast meat is on the rare side. Rare roasting the entire bird means the legs will probably be tough, but they can be recooked and used in other dishes. If the bird is stuffed with a regular stuffing, it must be cooked to well-done since it has to roast longer to bring the internal temperature up. Stuffing is often baked separately and the bird's cavity filled with apple or orange, onion, celery, and herbs for flavor and moisture.

When roasting ducks or geese, brush the birds first with olive oil or melted butter and/or lay slices of bacon or salt pork across the breast. Pieces of cold, seasoned butter may also be pushed under the breast skin. Or, roast the bird breast-side down until the last half hour, then turn it over and drape the breast with bacon or salt pork.

General Guide for Roasting

Geese

- Four pound, dressed, young bird, cooked rare: Roast at 450 for 15 to 20 minutes.
- Six to eight pound, dressed, stuffed young bird, cooked well done: Roast at 350 for 20 to 25 minutes per pound.
- Ten pounds and up, dressed mature bird, cooked well done: Parboil half an hour, drain, fill with apples, onion, and celery. Add water to the bottom of the roasting pan and roast at 350 for 15 to 20 minutes per pound. Baste several times while roasting. Raise the heat to 475 the last 15 minutes to brown the bird. Add a glaze if desired.

Ducks

- Rare: Roast in a 450 to 500 degree oven for 15 to 20 minutes depending on the size of the duck.
- Medium: Simply reduce the oven temperature at this time to 350 and roast for another 20 minutes or less depending on the size and on how you like your duck. If it is stuffed, increase the total roasting time to an hour or more.

Birds and fruit have a natural affinity for each other and waterfowl is no exception. The rich, full flavors of these birds are enhanced when cooked or served with fruit in some form. Other than filling the cavity with fruit, consider chopped fruit in a stuffing, a fruit glaze or marinade, or serve the bird with a fruit sauce, chutney, or poached fruits.

Photo courtesy of M. Fleming

Seasoned Baked Ducks

A few words should be said for coots, shovelers, and the sea ducks, or fish ducks, such as mergansers, scoters, and buffleheads. They have a bad reputation for flavor and smell. Those who wish to try these birds might consider these ideas: soak the birds, or just the breasts, overnight in one tablespoon salt and one tablespoon soda to one quart of water, or in vinegar water. Drain and rinse, then cook them in a crock pot, long and slow. Be generous with seasonings and herbs.

Waterfowl are excellent on a charcoal grill. A favorite recipe starts with filleting duck or goose breast meat. Split the breast meat in half, cutting almost the length of a fillet. Open out flat and soak the fillet in salt water for a couple of hours. Drain and season them with season salt, add one can of thawed condensed orange juice, and soak for four to five hours. Roll up fillets and wrap strips of bacon around them. Hold with toothpicks. Cook medium rare over charcoal.

Special Recipes

Roast Goose in Apple Wine

1 wild goose	2 cups apple wine
1 large apple	2 bay leaves
1 large onion	6 peppercorns
Handful of celery leaves	10 juniper berries, crushed
$\frac{1}{2}$ tsp. of fresh ground	1 Tbsp. cornstarch
black pepper	$\frac{1}{4}$ cup cold water
$\frac{1}{2}$ tsp. ground sage	$\frac{1}{2}$ cup currant or
$\frac{1}{4}$ cup flour	apple jelly, melted

1 large oven cooking bag

Wash the goose well inside and dry with paper towels. Rub cavity with the sage and pepper. Quarter or halve the apple and onion and stuff into the cavity along with the celery leaves. Add the flour to the oven bag and holding the top closed, shake the bag to coat the inside with the flour. Add the wine to the bag and mix until blended with the flour. Add the bay leaves, peppercorns and juniper berries. Put the goose in the bag. Close with the tie and make several small slits in the top of the bag.

Roast in preheated 350 degree oven for 2 to 2½ hours. Raise the oven temperature to 475. Remove the goose to a jelly-roll pan, brush with the melted jelly, and return goose to the oven to glaze. Brush several times. Pour the juices from the bag into a pan and thicken with the water/cornstarch mix, stirring and cooking until thickened and clear.

Serves four or *more*.

Butterfly Duck

1 large wild duck	3 Tbsps. plum sauce
2 tsps. salt	or hoisin sauce
$\frac{1}{4}$ tsp. fresh ground black pepper	2 Tbsps. honey
$\frac{1}{2}$ tsp. 5-Spice powder	$\frac{1}{4}$ cup dry vermouth

large garlic cloves, finely minced

Wash and dry duck. Preheat oven to 425. Trim off any excess neck skin or extra fat, and cut off wings at the first joint. Using a sharp knife, cut the duck open lengthwise along the breast. Open it up and flatten by pressing down hard with hands, skin side of duck up. Place the duck in a roasting pan; pour two quarts of boiling water over it and let stand five minutes. Pour off the water and dry duck and pan.

199

Combine the salt, pepper, and 5-Spice powder in one small bowl; the plum sauce and garlic in another bowl. Rub both sides of the duck with the salt mixture. Rub the cavity side only with the garlic mixture. Place the duck on a rack in the roasting pan, cavity side down; add one cup hot water and roast for 35 minutes.

Combine honey and vermouth and heat. When duck is done drain off any fat from the pan with a bulb baster; raise the oven temperature to 475 and baste the duck generously with the honey glaze. Roast 15 minutes more, basting several times. Place the duck on a serving platter and garnish as desired.   *Serves two.*

Photo courtesy of M. Fleming

Curried Duck

Curried Duck
2 small wild ducks (or a goose), cut up

Cook the birds by whatever method you prefer. They may be baked, braised or fried. The sauce may be added the last few minutes of the cooking time, or added to the ducks after cooking, or served alongside as a side dish.

Curry Sauce
¼ cup butter or margarine
¼ cup packed brown sugar

1 Tbsp. curry powder (more or less to taste)
$\frac{1}{2}$ tsp. salt
$\frac{1}{2}$ tsp. pepper
1-2 tart apples, cored, pared, and chopped or sliced
1 onion, chopped
1 rib celery, chopped
$\frac{1}{2}$ cup raisins

Melt the butter or margarine in a large skillet, add the brown sugar and stir to dissolve. Add the curry powder, salt, and pepper; stir and cook a minute or two. Add the remaining ingredients and cook until the apples are limp.

Photo courtesy of M. Fleming

Duck in Cream Sauce

Ducks in Cream Sauce

1 or 2 wild ducks, cut up	**1 cup sliced fresh mushrooms**
Flour	**2 Tbsps. minced fresh parsley**
Salt and pepper	**$\frac{1}{2}$ tsp. crushed thyme leaves**
4 Tbsps. olive oil	**1 cup dry red wine**
1 onion, thinly sliced	**1 cup sour cream**

Preheat oven to 350. Sprinkle the duck with salt and pepper and dredge in flour. In a large Dutch oven, heat the oil and brown the meat on both sides. Add the onions and mushrooms and saute. Add all remaining ingredients except for the sour cream. Cover and bake 1½ hours or more until meat is tender. Reduce the oven temperature to 300 and stir in the sour cream. Bake another half hour.

Serves two to four.

Broiled Goose Supremes

Wash and dry the goose breasts well. Rub both sides with olive oil or melted butter, garlic powder and pepper. Place the breasts on a broiler rack on the broiler pan. Preheat the broiler and cook about four to five minutes three inches from the heat. Baste frequently with olive oil. Cook longer for less rare. Salt to taste. Good served with sauteed fresh mushrooms. Or baste them with:

¼ cup dry vermouth   **¼ cup melted butter**

Season with salt and pepper and sprinkle with minced parsley.

Duck Stuffed with Sauerkraut

**1 tart apple, cored, pared and
finely chopped
¼ cup chopped onion
2 garlic cloves, thinly sliced
1 tsp. caraway seeds
2 wild ducks
½ tsp. pepper
2 Tbsps. paprika
1 lb. 13 oz. can sauerkraut, drained
½ cup chopped celery**

Preheat oven to 500. Sprinkle the ducks inside and out with pepper and paprika. Combine the stuffing ingredients and stuff ducks; skewer closed. Place them on a rack in a roasting plan and add several cups of water and wine to the bottom of the pan. Roast for 15 minutes; reduce heat to 350 for the remainder of the time. Figure 35 minutes per pound judging by the largest duck. Brush with melted currant jelly and glaze if desired.

CHAPTER 13

CONSERVATION AND THE ETHICAL WATERFOWLER

> *Canvasback Ducks! Yes, canvasback ducks;*
> *and at this late date, you can form no idea of*
> *how plenty they were. Why, I have seen the sky*
> *darkened with them, the bay like the driven*
> *snow as their white backs glistened in the sun,*
> *and when they arose, it seemed like one con-*
> *tinuous roar of thunder. It was no trick to kill*
> *them, for they abounded in the countless*
> *thousands.*

The "late date" was 1890 when Robert Law, a Maryland conservationist, penned those words. He thought he was witnessing the low point of the continent's canvasback population. What would he say if he knew the hunter's most prized duck would continue to decline through the next century, until, finally, only a remnant remained and their hunting was suspended?

It's true that chimney smoke, rather than gunsmoke, caused the canvasback's demise, and the duck may indeed recover and thrive. But it can't be done without the help of sportsmen. The hunter's role has changed since those naive days of the taker, who thought the supply was limitless, who killed ducks by the hundreds, with no thought of where his actions would lead. Today's waterfowler knows better, and with that knowledge comes a responsibility to value the experience of taking a couple of ducks rather than a heavy bag, to conserve what remains, and in one way or another, to put back more than is taken.

Few men are more qualified to comment on today's waterfowl situation than another Maryland conservationist, Joseph P. Linduska. A waterfowl biologist and conservation writer for a halfcentury, he has written the following summary of the history and status of waterfowl conservation.

Photo courtsy U.S. Fish and Wildlife Service

**Overhunting was a contributing factor to the decline of waterfowl popula-
tions prior to the 1930s. Since then, responsible hunters have been the chief
contributors to the fight against waterfowl's biggest threat: disappearing
habitat.**

In the 1920s, recognition came hard for a 10-year-old in the rough-neck mining town of Butte, Montana. So I guarded with care a time-worn photo that I occasionally flashed among my grade-school buddies to prove that by bloodlines, at least, I had the right stuff.

Twenty years later, as a professional biologist, that same picture was seldom brought out—and then it was only with some embarrassment and lengthy explanation.

The photo was a hunting scene taken at Red Rock Lakes (now a National Wildlife Refuge) a good 150 miles from Butte. In the foreground stood my old man, his double-barrel with "ears" draped over one forearm. Alongside him were two partners and a huge Chesapeake Bay retriever (a very long way from "home").

Photo courtsy of R. L. Davis, Jr.

An ethical waterfowler knows the *effective* range of his load, can accurately judge when a duck or goose is in that range, and shoots only then.

In the background were double-hung barn doors festooned with every kind of water bird imaginable. The ducks, several layers deep, were too numerous to count. There were coots and shorebirds and geese. And, finally, there were several trumpeter swans, a species later so depleted that the refuge was created.

This picture tells a good deal about what has happened to waterfowling over one man's lifetime. Prior to a 1916 treaty between the United States and Canada, ducks and geese enjoyed little or no protection. In the few places where restraints were imposed by states, a 25-bird limit on ducks was not terribly confining. Pop's barn door of waterfowl were all legally taken and easy to come by. Today, his son's limits would hardly obscure the car's radiator.

But even Pop's time, good as it was, was not the best of all times. Beginning about 1840, city folks developed a taste for wild game and market hunting came into being. The new fad coincided with the extension of our railroad system and refrigerated cars. Wild game of all sorts was delivered to far-flung population centers. Within 50 years, many game species had been all but wiped out. Waterfowl were sharply reduced in numbers and a few, such as the wood duck, were driven to the point of extinction.

The Tragedy of Wetlands Draining

Had excesses of market hunting been the only factor decimating our migratory flocks, that would have been remedied through regulations and enforcement. But at the same time, other factors were at work. Our United States Congress, in its boneheadedness, passed a series of Swamp Land Acts that eventually led to the transfer of 65 million acres of swamp and overflow lands to 15 states. In turn, sweet-talking promoters wheedled these lands from corrupt or indifferent state governments for little or nothing. Most of this vast acreage was drained for agriculture or other purposes.

The drainage craze has never fully subsided; it continues today. Even more shameful than the Swamp Lands giveaway is that much of the drainage since then has actually been government subsidized.

What's happened to the ducks? Consider this. In the beginning, this nation possessed 215 million acres of wetlands-habitat for ducks and other water-dependent wildlife. Today, we have half that and the decline continues. In recent years (from the mid-1950s to the mid-1970s) 9 mil-

Habitat improvement and protection is the most important facet of waterfowl conservation.

lion acres were destroyed nationwide. Nearly 90 percent of this drainage occurred in the Southeast and involved 5.5 million acres of forested wetlands. Most of this, in turn, was bottomland hardwoods representing some of the most productive wildlife habitats in the United States.

Fragile Lives of Waterfowl

Beginning with the egg in the nest, many factors serve to diminish populations of wildfowl. Botulism can be a devastating killer and can account for thousands of birds in a few days time. Its effects are most commonly seen on the alkali marshes and lakes of the West. The Great Salt Lake includes such alkali flats and in 1932, an estimated 250,000 ducks died from this dread disease in that one area alone.

Fowl cholera is another killer of waterfowl. It, like botulism, can cut heavily into local populations of many species of waterbirds. As one example, Muleshoe National Wildlife Refuge in the winter of 1956-57 reported losing over 60,000 ducks to this disease.

Numerous other diseases and parasites take their toll. Beginning at the nest, the eggs are relished by a long list of predators; chicks fall prey to crows, hawks, owls and predatory fish such as bass and pike. Those lucky enough to survive all this may well be stricken down by a hailstorm. And then they fly the gauntlet south.

Eons of time have attuned them well to this constant attrition that, after all, is the lot of all living matter. What time has not prepared them for is how to live and multiply *without water.* The foxes and coyotes, botulism and hailstorms they can handle. Deny them their breeding grounds and their population will be decimated.

Biologists have learned in the past 50 years that habitat is the number-one requirement to producing and sustaining wildlife. It shouldn't have taken so long. As early as 1934 it was suggested that widespread drainage in the northern Great Plains might be a major cause in the decline of waterfowl. In retrospect, it was a dead-right conclusion. Since then we've learned that half of our duck crop in an average year is produced in the prairie pothole region. It covers most of south-central Canada, Minnesota, and the Dakotas.

What we've done to the U.S. portion of that big duck factory is scandalous. Between 1936 and 1963, over 6 million acres were drained for agriculture, much of it under government subsidy. About one-fourth was judged to be of significant value to waterfowl. Federally-assisted drainage alone claimed more than 250,000 acres from 1951 to 1954. As far back as 1964, an inventory showed only about 2.5 million acres remaining of our most productive wetlands in the three-state area mentioned. This wanton drainage continues to present, at a rate of 1 to 2 percent annually in the prairie states.

Today's population of prairie nesting birds (most of our choice ducks) reflects this devastation brought to the land by dragline and bulldozer. Geese have done better, primarily because their nesting areas in the icebound north are ill-suited to farming or other "useful" purposes. For most geese, adversity is reckoned in the supply of foxes and frozen or flooded nests. But these are transitory events, and years of bust are eventually followed by years of boom.

But following the drainage around the turn of the century came prolonged and widespread drought. During the "Dirty Thirties," most of the prairie potholes overlooked by the drainers were sucked dry by hot winds of a rainless decade or more. The birds (along with muskrats, mink, beaver, fish, and others) went into a further steep decline.

So catastrophic was the event that two biologists wrote this in 1934: "Serious drought conditions have arisen periodically throughout recorded history, always doubtless working hardships upon the waterfowl. But never, so far as is known, have there been so many destructive agencies and conditions at work at once upon a depleted waterfowl supply as during the past five years. During that period the number of waterfowl have fallen drastically."

The Fledgling Concept of Conservation

In a way this last insult to waterfowl may well have been to their long-term benefit. Public interest, which had begun on the subject, eventually reached the desk of President Franklin D. Roosevelt. He moved promptly to appoint a waterfowl committee made up of Jay N. "Ding" Darling, a famous cartoonist who had publicized the problem through his widely syndicated column; Aldo Leopold, professor and conservation leader (he was later to become the patron saint of modern game management); and Thomas Beck, a well-known publisher. These three

"Mallards Coming in for a Landing," drawn by "Ding" Darling, launched the Federal Duck Stamp program in 1934. Since then, the sale of nearly 100 million stamps has raised about $325 million to purchase 4 million acres of waterfowl habitat.

gave top priority to preservation of the breeding grounds and recommended a $50-million program to preserve and rehabilitate nesting marshes.

Roosevelt's next move was to appoint Darling as Chief of the Bureau of Biological Survey (now U.S. Fish and Wildlife Service) where he would have full responsibility to implement the program of restoration. A fledgling refuge system was already in place and Darling engaged a young biologist, whose energy and daring matched his own, to lead the refuge program of land acquisition and development.

These two, "Ding" Darling and biologist J. Clark Salyer II, threatened, cajoled, and pleaded with Congress and other government agencies for assistance. The Great Depression was on and, through Emergency Acts then existing, they obtained both money and consignments of workers. A rescue effort for waterfowl was finally underway.

Other substantial developments to benefit waterfowl came about in this era of the mid-1930s. In 1934, the Migratory Bird Hunting Stamp Act was passed; the first stamp was drawn by Darling. The "Duck Stamp," as it has come to be known, is required of all waterfowlers over

Photo courtesy of R. L. Davis, Jr.

State owned and maintained Wildlife Management Areas offer opportunities to hunters and habitat for wildlife.

Oil spills, habitat destruction, and other indirect human causes of water-fowl mortality probably take more ducks and geese than hunters.

the age of 16. The proceeds are used in purchase of wetlands. Since its inception, it has generated over $700 million to purchase 5.2 million acres of vital habitat.

Also in 1934, Congress passed the Fish and Wildlife Coordination Act. It, for the first time, gave recognition to wildlife and recreational values on water development projects and led to the establishment of a number of federal refuges.

The Federal Aid in Wildlife Restoration Act passed in 1937 deserves special mention. Commonly called "PR" after the bill's sponsors, Key Pittman of Nevada and Willis Robertson of Virginia, it receives all the money from an excise tax on the manufacturer's price of sporting arms and ammunition and several other hunting-related items. It also collects matching federal funds. Over its 50 years of existence, PR has allotted over $2 billion to the states for land and water acquisition, research, and management. All told, 4 million acres of critical wildlife habitat, in-cluding many wetlands, have been brought into public ownership.

Not only were the 1930s notable for landmark conservation legisla-tion, it was a period marked by widespread citizen involvement and the emergence of game management as a profession. This one 10-year span also saw the formation of Ducks Unlimited, which has raised many millions of dollars for the preservation of Canadian wetlands. The 1930s also gave birth to a Cooperative Wildlife Research Unit Program to meet the needs for trained professionals in the field.

With special pertinence for waterfowl hunters, *Migration of Birds* by Frederick C. Lincoln was published in 1935. This publication defined, for the first time, four major flyways for waterfowl and other birds: Pacific, Central, Mississippi, and Atlantic. A great deal of subsequent study has shown that Lincoln's flyways were not of the exclusive nature he envisioned. Yet, they were accurate enough to give basis to a revolutionary new means of hunter harvest. Previously, hunting had been managed by zones running horizontally across the country, a system of convenience and little more. Lincoln recognized separate populations within each flyway - flocks from a certain area on the breeding grounds. Management by flyways has permitted a far larger harvest of birds without risking overshooting, since it takes into account different hunting pressures and varying degrees of breeding success for each flyway.

Waterfowl Conservation Today

The waterfowl situation today stands in marked contrast to that at the start of this century. As for numbers of birds, we may never again see the flights commonplace to that day. Consider yourself lucky if, some years ahead, you can hunt under bag limits such as your father enjoyed 40 or more hunting seasons past.

A sustained program for acquisition and *preservation* of habitat is a priority item to ensure the future of waterfowl. U.S. and Canadian governments have taken the initiative with the North American Waterfowl Management Plan adopted in 1986. This far-reaching document provided a framework for waterfowl management and conservation on the continent through the year 2000. The plan set goals for waterfowl populations, identified habitat conservation needs, and outlined ways of solving administrative problems. The program does not provide any more funding for waterfowl conservation, however. It depends on the regular government, corporate, and private funding.

Today we have competent wildlife administrators who know what to do but who need support. They have strong allies in the form of private conservation organizations whose sole mission is the preservation of our natural surroundings. Some have the betterment of hunting as an objective; some have other motivations. Whatever the purpose, a wet acre saved for the marsh wren is an acre saved for the mallard. We all stand to gain. The key to success is citizen involvement. Hunters must give full support to these organized citizen groups that try to give ducks and geese the edge they need.

Given their different habits and places of nesting, waterfowl do not succeed or fail as a group. In any given year some may experience good production while others do well to break even. This factor, among others, is what makes harvest by species a biologically-sound procedure. It calls for skills in identification that many modern-day nimrods lack. The gunner of tomorrow will need to be a naturalist of sorts if he is to gain the full benefits of what regulations offer.

Photo courtesy U.S. Fish and Wildlife Service

Banding has been the most successful technique for monitoring waterfowl. Used by bird fanciers since the 1600s, bands became the Fed's main method of gathering duck data in 1920.

Today's waterfowl hunter appreciates the value of modern conservation measures. A single drake canvasback is a prized trophy.

A majority of hunters are observant of the law and ethical in their behavior. Some are not. It is no secret that disobedience of the laws and lack of sportsmanship in the field are the two elements of hunting that play most strongly into the hands of the anti-hunting bloc. Yes, hunters could find themselves denied some of the privileges of hunting by the determined actions of such groups. That much alone should be reason enough to keep ethics in hunting.

East Coast hunters of a generation back (at least those here on Chesapeake Bay) called it a wasted day if they didn't come in with four or five drake canvasbacks. Today, the can in these parts is an oddity. But the new generation of deep-water gunners don't miss what they never knew. Give them a mixed bag of ringnecks and bluebills and they've had a ball.

We'll be seeing more of this sort of thing. Species in greatest supply will have the more liberal regulations, and the new hunters will follow along, bringing with them the same enthusiasm that infected the hunters of yore. To the old-timers bowing out, the good old days were 20 or more years ago. But to the newcomer just getting waterfowl fever, the good days are now—whenever a pair of ducks, of most any species, are brought to bag.

214

Photo courtesy of R. L. Davis, Jr.

In most breeding areas, overall nesting success and survival depend on the conditions of wetlands. Each new brood pond that is built provides the critical habitat for a waterfowl family—and their future generations.

To the connoisseur of yesteryear, but a few ducks were fit to eat, namely: cans, mallards, blacks, and blue-winged teal. Yet in the lean times of the late '30s, I practically raised my second-born on coots and mergansers, the only birds that came the way of a shore-bound graduate student. My boy likes them to this day.

Years back, a similar experience was related to me by Willis Robertson (the same Robertson of PR fame). He was an ardent hunter of rails, but he returned one day with a pair of hooded mergansers which he "generously" presented to his gardener. On seeing him the next day, the Senator asked how he liked the ducks. The lad replied, "Boss, I like fish and I like fowl, but that's the first time I ever had both in the same piece of meat."

It's like Pop said of his last few hunts: "Waterfowling is shot."

I think so, too.

My son says it's the greatest sport in the world and here to stay.

My son is right. There will be changes, as in everything else there is change, but a love of nature is as deeply rooted in Americans today as it was in all our forebears. There will be no Silent Fall. We can and will do whatever it takes to assure that our autumn skies are alive with the calls of these great migrant flocks. Waterfowling in the future may well be different, but because of sportsmen, it will *be*.

215

Waterfowl Hunting Ethics

Hunting ethics encompass all the responsibilities a hunter has to other hunters, landowners, the general public, and the game. Governments require certain generally accepted ethical behavior through hunting laws and regulations. In other cases, the hunter himself has the obligation to decide what is right, what is wrong, and hunt according to those standards.

Some ethical questions are simple; others are more complex. Most ethical questions can be resolved by answering the questions, is it legal or is it fair to everyone concerned, including the game and myself? There are standards to follow, but ultimately, you must decide.

Responsibility to Other Hunters

Besides safety, you have several other responsibilities to your fellow hunters. If you find another hunter where you planned to hunt, bow out. Moving in on another hunter is not only discourteous and unfair, but also unsafe and counterproductive; it's likely neither of you will get a duck and you'll both have a bad experience. Give respect to your fellow hunter, and hopefully one day you'll be on the receiving end.

Try to pass on responsible hunting behavior to fellow hunters. If a new hunter seems to be going astray, try to educate him in hunting ethics. If a companion refuses to hunt responsibly, refuse to hunt with him.

Don't litter, drive vehicles where others may be hunting, or otherwise disturb other people or the area. Most hunters have deep feelings for nature and the peace of mind they find while hunting. Don't violate them.

Responsibilities to Landowners

One example of how hunters hurt themselves through poor ethics is the alienation of landowners. Each year, thousands of acres of private land are posted off limits because hunters treated the land or its owner with disrespect. It hurts all hunters.

Always get permission before hunting on any private property. Approach the landowner with courtesy—not only because you will have a better chance of getting permission, but to promote the image of the hunter. Once you receive permission, treat the land with the utmost care. Leave no signs you were there—take spent shells and litter with you, and maybe pick up some litter left by others. Don't drive on soft ground and leave tire ruts.

Other ways to keep good landowner relations are to avoid disturbing livestock, fences, crops, and other property. Don't abuse your welcome by bringing a carload of companions or hunting on the land day after day.

A token of appreciation such as a gift, a card, or an offer to help with chores goes a long way toward being welcome the next year.

Responsibilities to the Public

Remember that the environment and animals belong to everyone, not just hunters. Respect the rights of people who enjoy nature without hunting—avoid shooting in areas where you know non-hunters are enjoying the outdoors. Keep shell cases and other signs of hunting out of view. Don't display bagged animals to people who may not want to see them. Remember that unfavorable public opinion has resulted in laws and regulations of adverse impact to hunters.

Another duty the hunter owes the public is to ensure the enforcement of all laws. Hunters must abide by the laws and report those who trespass, poach animals, shoot road signs, or otherwise vandalize property.

Responsibility to the Game

Waterfowl, like all game animals, deserve the greatest respect and most humane treatment a hunter can give his prey. Hunters who do not feel a certain reverence for a duck or goose and an obligation to conserve the resource are missing the essence of hunting.

Never take a shot that has a strong chance of crippling. Under no circumstances should you shoot indiscriminately into a flock. Always identify your target. Of course, never exceed bag limits or use unsportsmanlike hunting methods.

Responsibilities to Yourself

Finally, don't forget your responsibilities to yourself. If a certain law or hunting regulation conflicts with your well-considered ethical beliefs, work to change that law. Fight it with letters and votes, not disobedience.

Don't take a chance or violate your ethics in a way that you may regret later. By the same token, hunt hard, hunt honestly, and be proud of your sportsmanship.

Pass Along the Tradition

If you're a hunter in the truest sense, you will eventually reach a point where you you derive the most hunting satisfaction from introducing others to the sport.

Most hunters are eager to take their young children hunting. Some of those potential hunters, however, are ruined by an overanxious and insensitive parent, and never show any further desire to hunt. Picture yourself a little scared, a lot cold, wet, sleepy, and bored, and being chastised by an adult for four hours. Once would be more than enough.

Here are some suggestions: At first, choose evening hunts on mild days. Be prepared to sacrifice some shooting, so that the child can poke his or her head out of the blind to see the ducks cupping their wings. Gently, simply, and with enthusiasm explain how things work and how things are done in duck hunting. If the child is old enough, he or she may be allowed to have a BB gun and imagine participation in the hunt.

Children old enough to handle a shotgun should be started with a 20-gauge (not a .410) with proper fit. Teach them shooting skills with clay targets—straightaway shots are easier, and a few hits will build the child's confidence. On the first hunting trip, try to set up the easiest shots on game, also.

Talk with the child about hunting responsibilities and ethics that all hunters should abide. About showing respect for game by never taking a chancy shot, by making every effort to recover a wounded animal, and by never wasting bagged game. Make him or her realize why they must also treat landowners and the general public with respect, to prevent prejudice against hunters.

Instruct the child early on conservation, safety, and ethical aspects, too, because they—along with the child hunter—are the future of our waterfowling heritage.

Photo courtesy of M. Fleming

Teaching our youth to appreciate waterfowl and its pursuit is the key to the future of the sport.

Appendix

Photo courtesy of M. Fleming

THE NRA AND HUNTING

T he National Rifle Association encourages and supports sport hunting through a wide variety of programs and services.

The NRA Hunter Services Department assists state and provincial hunter education programs with support materials and training programs for professional and volunteer staff. The NRA Hunter Clinic Program answers the demand for advanced hunter education by providing clinics emphasizing skills, responsibility, and safety as applied to hunting techniques and specific game species. NRA Hunter Clinic Instructors are provided with detailed teaching tools and up-to-date educational resources to aid in expanding their students' abilities. The NRA Youth Hunter Education Challenge offers a series of events on the local, state, and national levels to challenge young hunters, through hunting-simulated events, to apply basic skills learned in the classroom.

The NRA Institute for Legislative Action protects the legal rights of hunters. NRA publications provide a variety of printed material on firearms, equipment, and techniques for hunters, including *American Hunter* magazine, the largest periodical in the U.S. devoted to hunting. Junior programs encourage young people to participate in hunting. Special insurance benefits are available to NRA hunting members, and hunters can further benefit by joining an NRA hunting club or by affiliating an existing club with the NRA. The NRA works with other hunting organizations to sustain a positive image of hunting as a traditional form of recreation, to combat anti-hunting efforts, and to promote a life-long interest in hunting.

For further information, contact the Hunter Services Department, National Rifle Association, 11250 Waples Mill Road, Fairfax, VA 22030. (703) 267-1524.

NATIONAL RIFLE ASSOCIATION
OF AMERICA

The National Rifle Association of America was founded in New York in 1871 "for the improvement of its members in marksmanship." From this modest beginning, the NRA has evolved into a nationwide, nonprofit organization with a membership in the millions.

Today, the NRA is a nationwide educational, recreational, and public service organization dedicated to the rights of responsible citizens to own and use firearms for recreation and defense.

The NRA is a nonprofit corporation supported entirely by its membership and affiliated clubs. It is not affiliated with any arms or ammunition manufacturers nor with any commercial firearm businesses and receives no appropriations from Congress. The NRA cooperates with all the branches of the U.S. armed forces, federal agencies, and state and local governments interested in teaching firearm marksmanship, safety, and hunting skills to all interested persons.

The NRA has long recognized the importance of hunters in its fight to protect our right to keep and bear arms. Because hunters comprise a vast segment of the gun owning public, the image they project reflects on all gun owners. The NRA has worked to promote safe and responsible conduct by hunters in the field since its beginning more than a century ago.

The NRA believes that well managed hunting is a beneficial use of renewable wildlife resources, which, when left to nature, are lost to predation, disease, starvation, or old age. Proper hunting is in complete accord with the moral tenets and historical facts of human existence. The hunting heritage predates recorded history by many centuries. The hunter's participation in the chase today is a healthy exercise, both physically and spiritually.

The hunter's interest in wildlife has been the principal factor in fostering sound management and conservation practices. The commitment of hunters and the funds they provide through special taxes and licenses safeguards the future of all wildlife species.

Hunting is dominant among American traditions and has contributed substantially to our strong national character. Its future is a primary concern of the National Rifle Association.

To join NRA today, or for additional information regarding membership, please call 1-800-368-5714.

Photo courtesy of R. L. Davis, Jr.

NRA MATERIALS FOR
THE WATERFOWL HUNTER

The following are available from the NRA Program Materials Center and can help you prepare for your next hunt. To order any of the materials listed below, telephone (800) 336-7402 or order online at http://materials.nrahq.org/go/.

Description

NRA Hunter Skills Series
  Wild Turkey Hunting
  Whitetail Deer Hunting
  Waterfowl Hunting
  Muzzleloader Hunting
  Bowhunting
  Upland Bird Hunting
  Western Big Game Hunting

NRA Hunter Educational Brochures Series
  Turkey Hunting Safety
  Wild Game from Field to Table
  Firearms Safety and the Hunter
  Landowner Relations
  Responsible Hunting
  Hypothermia
  Fitness and Nutrition
  Water Safety
  Tree Stand Safety
  Hunting's Future? It's Up to You
  Eye and Ear Care
  Hunting and Wildlife Management
  Lyme Disease

THE NRA HUNTER SKILLS SERIES

The NRA Hunter Skills Series is a developing library of books on hunting, shooting, and related activities. It supports the NRA Hunter Clinic Program, a national network of seminars conducted by the NRA Hunter Services Department and independent hunter clinic instructors.

The hunter training manuals are developed by NRA staff, with the assistance of noted hunting experts, hunter educators, experienced outdoor writers, and representatives of hunting/conservation organizations. The publications are available in student (paperback) editions.

The program is planned to include clinics and support material on hunting whitetail deer, waterfowl, wild turkey, small game, predators, upland game, western big game, and others. It will also address marksmanship and hunting with rifle, shotgun, muzzleloader, handgun, and archery equipment.

For more information about the NRA Hunter Clinic Program and its training materials, contact NRA Hunter Services Department, 11250 Waples Mill Road, Fairfax, VA 22030. Telephone (703) 267-1516.

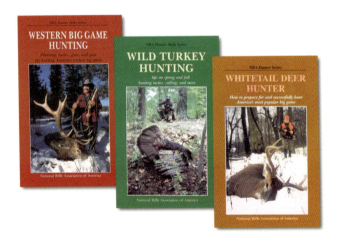

DUCKS
AT A
DISTANCE
A WATERFOWL IDENTIFICATION
GUIDE

Identification is Important

Identifying waterfowl gives many hours of enjoyment to millions of people. This guide will help you recognize birds on the wing—it emphasizes their fall and winter plumage patterns as well as size, shape, and flight characteristics. It does not include local names.

Recognizing the species of ducks and geese can be rewarding to birdwatchers and hunters—and the ducks.

Hunters can contribute to their own sport by not firing at those species that are either protected or scarce, and needed as breeders to restore the flocks. It can add to their daily limit; when extra birds of certain species can be taken legally, hunters who know their ducks on the wing come out ahead.

Knowing a mallard from a merganser has another side: gourmets prefer a corn-fed mallard to the fish duck.

What to Look For

Differences in size, shape, plumage patterns and colors, wing beat, flocking behavior, voice, and habitat—all help to distinguish one species from another.

Flock maneuvers in the air are clues. Mallards, pintails, and wigeon form loose groups; teal and shovelers flash by in small, compact bunches; at a distance, canvasbacks shift from waving lines to temporary V's.

Closer up, individual silhouettes are important. Variations of head shapes and sizes, lengths of wings and tails, and fat bodies or slim can be seen.

Within shotgun range, color areas can be important. Light conditions might make them look different, but their size and location are positive keys. The sound of their wings can help as much as their calls. Flying goldeneyes make a whistling sound; wood ducks move with a swish; canvas-backs make a steady rushing sound. Not all ducks quack; many whistle, squeal, or grunt.

Although not a hard and fast rule, different species tend to use different types of habitat. Puddle ducks like shallow marshes and creeks while divers prefer larger, deeper, and more open waters.

| Flock Pattern | Silhouette | Notable Features | Sound |

Eclipse Plumage

Drake: Spring Plumage

Hen

Drakes Emerging from Eclipse

Drake: Full Eclipse

Most ducks shed their body feathers twice each year. Nearly all drakes lose their bright plumage after mating, and for a few weeks resemble females. This hen-like appearance is called the eclipse plumage. The return to breeding coloration varies in species and individuals of each species. Blue-winged teal and shovelers may retain the eclipse plumage until well into the winter.

Wing feathers are shed only once a year; wing colors are always the same.

Drake: Fall Plumage

Puddle Ducks

Puddle ducks are typically birds of fresh, shallow marshes and rivers rather than of large lakes and bays. They are good divers, but usually feed by dabbling or tipping rather than submerging.

The speculum, or colored wing patch, is generally iridescent and bright, and often a telltale field mark.

Any duck feeding in croplands will likely be a puddle duck, for most of this group are sure-footed and can walk and run well on land. Their diet is mostly vegetable, and grain-fed mallards or pintails or acorn-fattened wood ducks are highly regarded as food.

Feeding   Takeoff

Mallard

Length—24"
Weight—2¾ lbs.

Eclipse Drake

Hen

The mallard is our most common duck, found in all flyways. The males are often called "greenheads." The main wintering area is the lower Mississippi basin, and along the gulf coast, but many stay as far north as open waters permit.

Hen   Drake

Drake

Drake

Hen

Flocks often feed in early morning and late afternoon in nearby harvested fields, returning to marshes and creeks to spend the night.

Drake

Hen

The flight is not particularly rapid. Hens have a loud *quack*; the drake's voice is a low-pitched *kwek-kwek*.

Typical Flock Pattern

Pintail

Length—26″
Weight—1¾ lbs.

Eclipse Drake

Hen

These ducks use all four flyways, but are most plentiful in the west.

They are extremely graceful and fast fliers, fond of zig-zagging from great heights before leveling off to land.

The long neck and tail make them appear longer than mallards, but in body size and weight they are smaller.

Hen   Drake

Drake

Drake

Hen

Drake

Hen

They are agile on land and often feed in grain fields. The drakes whistle; the hens have a coarse *quack*.

Typical Flock Pattern

Gadwall

Length—21"
Weight—2 lbs.

Eclipse Drake

Hen

Gadwalls are most numerous in the Central Flyway, but not too common anywhere. They are often called "gray mallards" or "gray ducks." They are one of the earliest migrants, seldom facing cold weather.

They are the only puddle ducks with a white speculum.

Hen   Drake

Drake

Drake

Hen

Small, compact flocks fly swiftly, usually in a direct line. Wingbeats are rapid.

Drakes whistle and *kack-kack*; hens *quack* like a mallard, but softer.

Drake

Typical Flock Pattern

Hen

Wigeon

Length—21″
Weight—1 ¾ lbs.

Eclipse Drake

Hen

These are nervous birds, quick to take alarm. Their flight is fast, irregular, with many twists and turns. In a bunched flock, their movements have been compared to those of pigeons.

When open water is handy, wigeons often raft up off-shore until late afternoon when they move to marshes and ponds to feed.

Hen   Drake

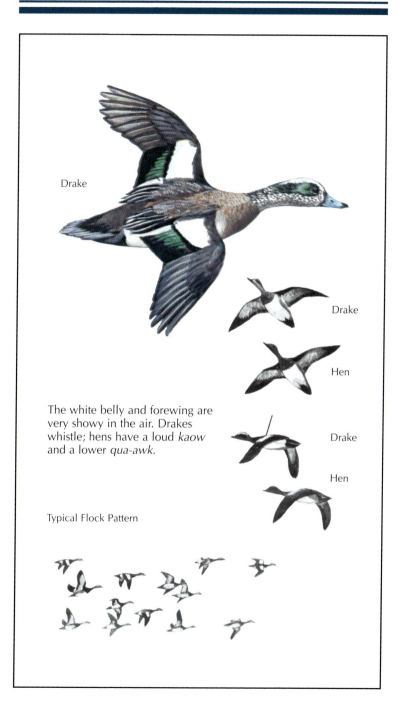

Drake

Drake

Hen

The white belly and forewing are very showy in the air. Drakes whistle; hens have a loud *kaow* and a lower *qua-awk*.

Drake

Hen

Typical Flock Pattern

Shoveler

Length—19 ½″
Weight—1 ½ lbs.

Eclipse Drake

Hen

Shovelers, "spoonbills" to many, are early migrants, moving out at the first frost. The largest numbers are in the Central and Pacific flyways.

The usual flight is steady and direct. When startled, the small flocks twist and turn in the air like teal.

Hen   Drake

Drake

Drake

Hen

They are not highly regarded as table birds, because one third of the usual diet is animal matter.

Drake

Hen

Drakes call *woh-woh* and *took-took*; the hen's *quack* is feeble.

Typical Flock Pattern

Blue-winged Teal

Length—16″
Weight—15 oz.

Hen

Eclipse Drake

Drake

Hen

Their small size and twisting, turning flight give the illusion of great speed. The small, compact flocks commonly fly low over the marshes, and often take the hunter by surprise. They are more vocal than most ducks—their high-pitched peeping and nasal quacking is commonly heard in spring and to a lesser extent in fall.

These teal are among the first ducks to migrate each fall, and one of the last in the spring.

Drake

Hen

Hen   Drake

Cinnamon Teal

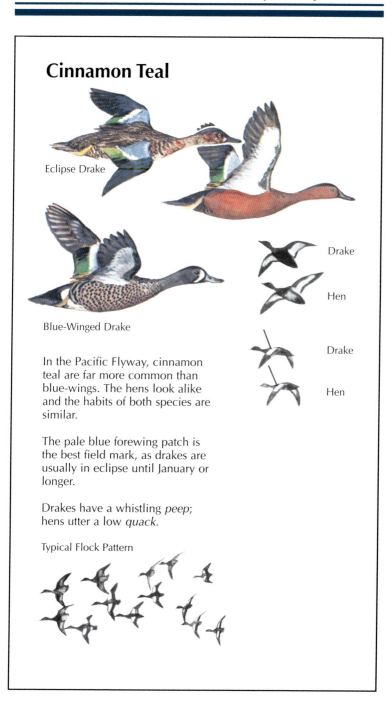

Eclipse Drake

Blue-Winged Drake

Drake

Hen

Drake

Hen

In the Pacific Flyway, cinnamon teal are far more common than blue-wings. The hens look alike and the habits of both species are similar.

The pale blue forewing patch is the best field mark, as drakes are usually in eclipse until January or longer.

Drakes have a whistling *peep*; hens utter a low *quack*.

Typical Flock Pattern

Green-Winged Teal

Length—15"
Weight—14 oz.

Eclipse Drake

Hen

Quite hardy—some birds stay as far north as open water is found.

The smallest and one of the most common of our ducks. Their tiny size gives the impression of great speed, but mallards can fly faster. Their flight is often low, erratic, with the entire flock twisting and turning as one unit.

Hen   Drake

Drake

Drake

Hen

They nest as far north as Alaska, and migrate in all four flyways. Early fall drakes are usually still in full eclipse plumage.

Drake

Drakes whistle and twitter; hens have a slight *quack*.

Hen

Typical Flock Pattern

245

Wood Duck

Length—18 ½″
Weight—1 ½ lbs.

Eclipse Drake

Hen

Found in all flyways; most numerous in the Atlantic and Mississippi flyways and fewest in the Central.

They are early migrants; most of them have left the northern States by mid-November.

Frequents wooded streams and ponds; perches in trees. Flies through thick timber with speed and ease and often feeds on acorns, berries, and grapes on the forest floors.

Hen   Drake

Drake

Drake

Hen

Flight is swift and direct;
flocks are usually small.

In the air, their wings make a
rustling, swishing sound.
Drakes call *hoo-w-ett*, often in
flight; hens have a *cr-r-ek*
when frightened.

Drake

Hen

Typical Flock Pattern

247

Black Duck

Length—24"
Weight—2 ¾ lbs.

Eclipse Drake

Hen

Drake

Similar Sexes

Typical Flock Pattern

A bird of the eastern States, primarily the Atlantic Flyway and, to a lesser extent, the Mississippi.

Shy and wary, regarded as the wariest of all ducks.

Often seen in company of mallards, but along the Atlantic coast frequents the salt marshes and ocean much more than mallards.

Flight is swift, usually in small flocks.

White wing lining in contrast to very dark body plumage is a good identification clue.

The hen's *quack* and the drake's *kwek-kwek* are duplicates of the mallard's.

Hen

Drake

Diving Ducks

Diving ducks frequent the larger, deeper lakes and rivers, and coastal bays and inlets.

The colored wing patches of these birds lack the brilliance of the speculums of puddle ducks. Since many of them have short tails, their huge, paddle feet may be used as rudders in flight, and are often visible on flying birds. When launching into flight, most of this group patter along the water before becoming airborne.

They feed by diving, often to considerable depths. To escape danger, they can travel great distances underwater, emerging only enough to show their head before submerging again.

Their diets of fish, shellfish, mollusks, and aquatic plants make them second choice, as a group, for sportsmen. Canvasbacks and redheads fattened on eel grass or wild celery are notable exceptions.

Since their wings are smaller in proportion to the size and weight of their bodies, they have a more rapid wing-beat than puddle ducks.

Takeoff

Feeding

Landing

Canvasback

Length—22"
Weight—3 lbs.

Hen

Eclipse Drake

Normally late to start south, canvasbacks migrate in lines and irregular V's.

In feeding areas, compact flocks fly in indefinite formations. Their wingbeat is rapid and noisy; their speed is the swiftest of all our ducks.

Hen   Drake

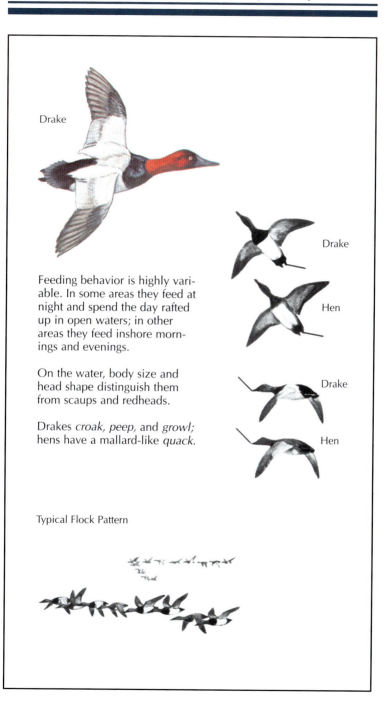

Drake

Drake

Hen

Drake

Hen

Feeding behavior is highly variable. In some areas they feed at night and spend the day rafted up in open waters; in other areas they feed inshore mornings and evenings.

On the water, body size and head shape distinguish them from scaups and redheads.

Drakes *croak, peep,* and *growl;* hens have a mallard-like *quack.*

Typical Flock Pattern

Redheads

Length—20″
Weight—2 ½ lbs.

Eclipse Drake

Hen

Range coast to coast, with the largest numbers in the Central Flyway. Migratory flocks travel in V's; move in irregular formations over feeding areas. Often found associating with canvasback.

In the air, they give the impression of always being in a hurry.

Hen   Drake

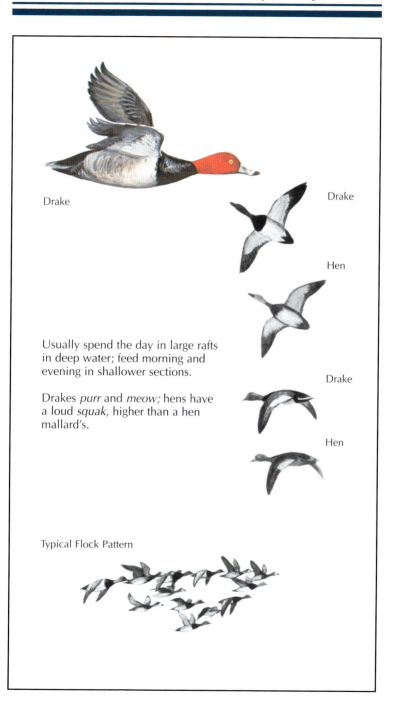

Drake

Drake

Hen

Usually spend the day in large rafts
in deep water; feed morning and
evening in shallower sections.

Drake

Drakes *purr* and *meow;* hens have
a loud *squak,* higher than a hen
mallard's.

Hen

Typical Flock Pattern

253

Ringneck

Length—17"
Weight—2 ½ lbs.

Eclipse Drake

Hen

Similar in appearance to scaups, but more often found in fresh marshes and wooded ponds. In flight, the dark wings are different from the white-edged wings of scaup.

Faint brown ring on drake's neck never shows in the field; light bands at tip and base of bill are conspicuous.

Hen   Drake

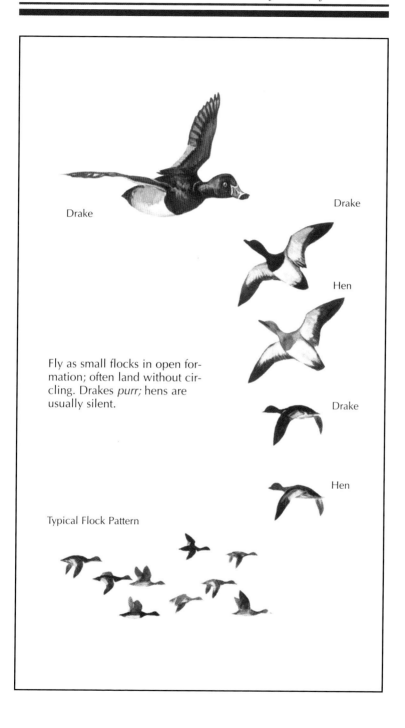

Drake

Drake

Hen

Fly as small flocks in open formation; often land without circling. Drakes *purr;* hens are usually silent.

Drake

Hen

Typical Flock Pattern

255

Scaup

Greater— Length—18 ½"
            Weight—2 lbs.

  Lesser— Length—17"
            Weight—1 ⅞ lbs.

Hen

Eclipse Drake

Except for the wing marks, greater and lesser scaup appear nearly identical in the field.

The light band near the trailing edges of the wings runs almost to the tip in the greater scaup, but only about half way in the lesser.

Greater scaup prefer large open water areas; lesser scaup often use marshes and ponds.

Lesser   Greater

Hen   Hen

Drake   Drake

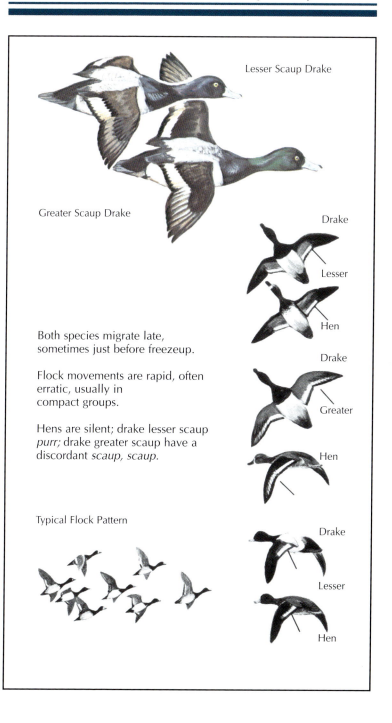

Lesser Scaup Drake

Greater Scaup Drake

Drake

Lesser

Hen

Both species migrate late, sometimes just before freezeup.

Drake

Flock movements are rapid, often erratic, usually in compact groups.

Greater

Hens are silent; drake lesser scaup *purr;* drake greater scaup have a discordant *scaup, scaup.*

Hen

Typical Flock Pattern

Drake

Lesser

Hen

257

Goldeneye

Common—Length—19″
        Weight—2 ¼ lbs.

Barrow's— Length—19″
        Weight—2 ¾ lbs.

Hen Both Species

Common Eclipse Drake

These are active, strong-winged fliers moving singly or in small flocks, often high in the air. Distinctive wing-whistling sound in flight has earned the name of whistlers.

Goldeneyes generally move south late in the season; most of them winter on coastal waters and the Great Lakes. Inland, they like rapids and fast water.

Barrow's   Common

Hen   Drake   Hen   Drake

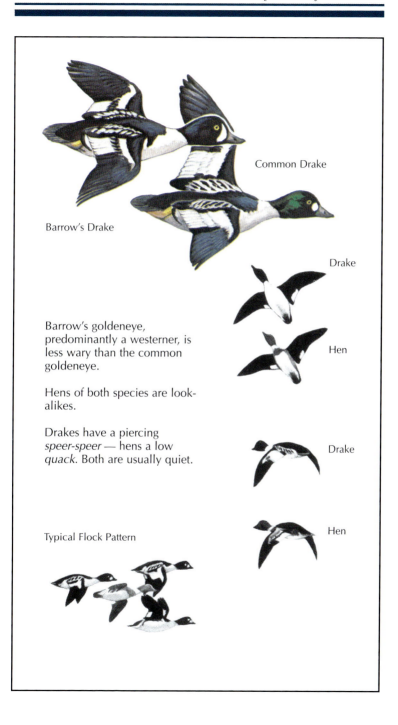

Common Drake

Barrow's Drake

Drake

Hen

Barrow's goldeneye, predominantly a westerner, is less wary than the common goldeneye.

Hens of both species are look-alikes.

Drakes have a piercing *speer-speer* — hens a low *quack*. Both are usually quiet.

Drake

Hen

Typical Flock Pattern

259

Bufflehead

Length—14 ½"
Weight—1 lbs.

Hen

Eclipse Drake

Stragglers migrate south in mid-fall, but the largest numbers move just ahead of freezeup. Most flocks in feeding areas are small—5 or 6 birds, with more hens and immatures than adult drakes.

Very small size, bold black and white color pattern, and low, swift flight are field marks. Unlike most divers, they can fly straight up from a watery takeoff.

Hen   Drake

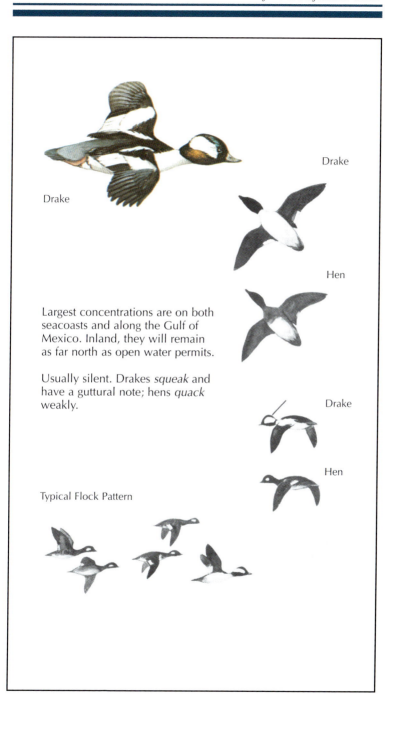

Drake

Drake

Hen

Largest concentrations are on both seacoasts and along the Gulf of Mexico. Inland, they will remain as far north as open water permits.

Usually silent. Drakes *squeak* and have a guttural note; hens *quack* weakly.

Drake

Hen

Typical Flock Pattern

Ruddy

Length—15 ½"
Weight—1 ⅓ lbs.

Winter Drake

Hen

The ruddy duck often dives or swims away from
danger rather than flying. When flying, their
small wings stroke so fast they resemble bumble-
bees.

Sexes Similar

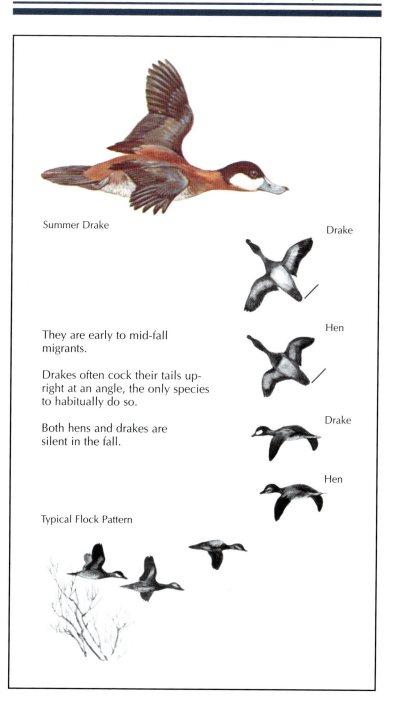

Summer Drake

Drake

Hen

Drake

Hen

They are early to mid-fall migrants.

Drakes often cock their tails upright at an angle, the only species to habitually do so.

Both hens and drakes are silent in the fall.

Typical Flock Pattern

Red-Breasted Merganser

Length—23″
Weight—2 ½ lbs.

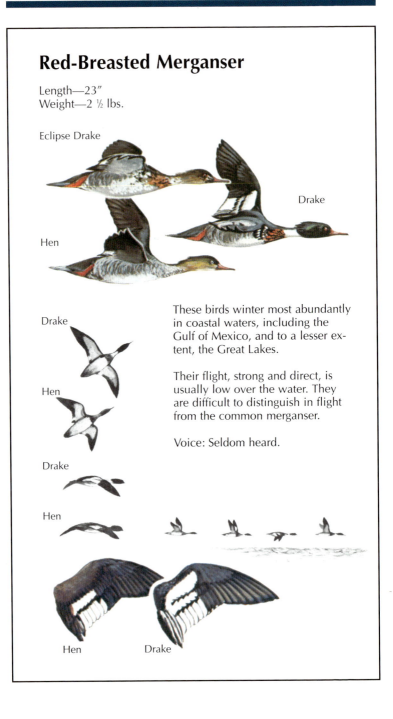

Eclipse Drake

Drake

Hen

These birds winter most abundantly in coastal waters, including the Gulf of Mexico, and to a lesser extent, the Great Lakes.

Their flight, strong and direct, is usually low over the water. They are difficult to distinguish in flight from the common merganser.

Voice: Seldom heard.

Drake

Hen

Drake

Hen

Hen   Drake

Common Merganser

Length—25 ½"
Weight—2 ½ lbs.

Eclipse Drake

Drake

Hen

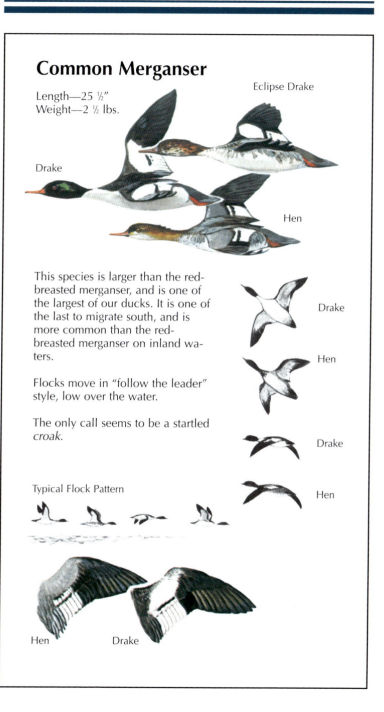

This species is larger than the red-breasted merganser, and is one of the largest of our ducks. It is one of the last to migrate south, and is more common than the red-breasted merganser on inland waters.

Drake

Hen

Flocks move in "follow the leader" style, low over the water.

Drake

The only call seems to be a startled *croak*.

Hen

Typical Flock Pattern

Hen   Drake

Hooded Merganser

Length—18″
Weight—1 ½ lbs.

Eclipse Drake

Drake

Hen

Drake

Hen

Drake

Hen

Often seen in pairs, or very small flocks. Short rapid wingstrokes create an impression of great speed.

Winters in the inland waters of all coastal States; seldom goes to salt water.

Voice: Seldom heard in fall.

Hen

Drake

Whistling Ducks

Length—18–19″
Weight—1 ¾ lbs.

Fulvous

Black-Bellied

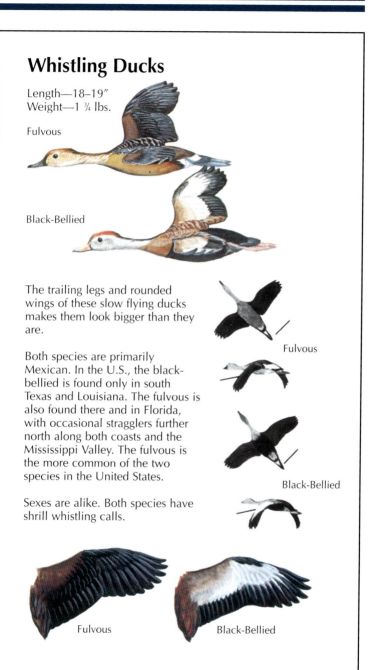

The trailing legs and rounded wings of these slow flying ducks makes them look bigger than they are.

Fulvous

Both species are primarily Mexican. In the U.S., the black-bellied is found only in south Texas and Louisiana. The fulvous is also found there and in Florida, with occasional stragglers further north along both coasts and the Mississippi Valley. The fulvous is the more common of the two species in the United States.

Black-Bellied

Sexes are alike. Both species have shrill whistling calls.

Fulvous   Black-Bellied

White-Winged Scoter

Length—21 ½"
Weight—3 ½ lbs.

The three scoters on these two pages are sea ducks, wintering on open coastal waters. White-wings are among the heaviest and largest of all ducks.

Surf Scoter

Length—19 ½"
Weight—2 lbs.

Like all scoters, these birds move along our coasts in loose flocks, stringing into irregular, wavy lines. Drakes can be distinguished from other scoters by two white patches on their head and the bright color of the bill.

Flight is strong, direct, usually close to the waves.

Black Scoter

Length—19 ½"
Weight—2 ½ lbs.

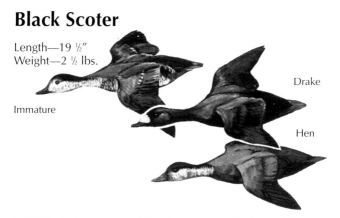

Immature

Drake

Hen

In flight, drakes appear all black except for the flash of the slight gray underwing and the bright yellow swelling at the base of the upper bill.

Scoters feed on mollusks, crabs, and some fish and very little vegetation. They are locally known as "coots."

Common Eider

Length—23 ½"
Weight—5 lbs.

Eclipse Drake

Drake

Hen

Thick-necked stocky birds, alternately flapping and sailing in flight; flocks string out in a line, close to the water. Found in the United States chiefly along New England coasts and occasionally south to New Jersey.

Other eiders—king, spectacled and Stellar's—occur in Alaska and are not pictured in this guide. King eiders occasionally are found in north Atlantic coastal waters.

Oldsquaw

Length—20 ½"
Weight—2 lbs.

Winter Drake

Summer Drake

Winter Hen

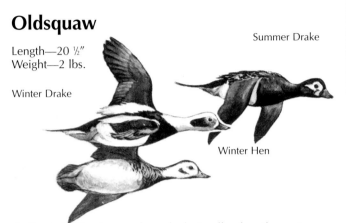

A slim, brightly plumaged sea duck. Smaller than the scoters or eiders.

Flight is swift and low with constantly changing flock formations. Ranges along both coasts and the Great Lakes.

One of the most vocal of ducks; drakes have a loud pleasant *caloo, caloo,* constantly heard.

Harlequin

Length—17"
Weight—1 ½ lbs.

Drake

Eclipse Drake

Hen

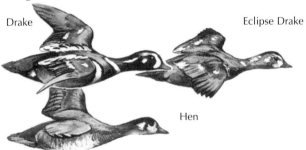

Glossy slate-blue plumage enlivened by white stripes and spots give the adult male harlequin a striking appearance. The female resembles a small female scoter. At a distance, both sexes look black. Flight is swift, with abrupt turns. Flocks are small and compact. Ranges both coasts, north from New Jersey and San Francisco. Uncommon.

Swans

Trumpeter— Length—59″
         Weight—28 lbs.
Whistling— Length—52″
         Weight—16 lbs.

Trumpeter

Immature: Both Species

Whistling

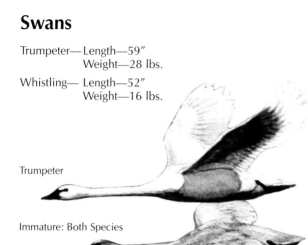

Once thought to be rare, trumpeter swans are slowly increasing in Alaska and on western refuges and parks.

Whistling swans are common and increasing. They winter near Chesapeake Bay, San Francisco Bay, Puget Sound and Salton Sea. Occasionally found in fields.

Both species are large with pure white plumage.

Canada Geese

Numerous and popular, Canada geese are often called "honkers." Includes several races varying in weight from 3 to over 12 pounds.

All have black heads and necks, white cheeks, similar habitats and voices. Sexes are identical.

Brant

Length—24–25"
Weight—3 ¼–3 ¾ lbs.

Black Brant

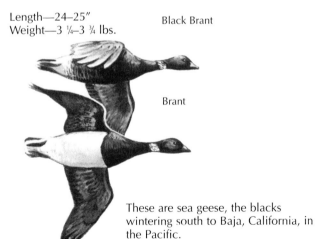

Brant

These are sea geese, the blacks wintering south to Baja, California, in the Pacific.

The Atlantic race winters from Virginia northward.
Flight is swift, in irregular and changing flock patterns.

Snow Geese

Immature

Adult

Immature
Blue

Adult
Blue

Length—29–31"
Weight—6 ½–7 ½ lbs.

Two races
of snow geese are
recognized: greater snows
along the Atlantic Coast, and
lesser snows elsewhere on the
continent. Blue geese are a
color phase of the lesser snow.

White-Fronted Geese

Length—29"
Weight—6 ¼ lbs.

Immature

Adult

Migrates chiefly in the Central and Pacific
flyways but also present in the Mississippi.
Rare in the Atlantic Flyway. Appears brownish gray
at a distance. Often called "specklebelly".

Most distinctive characteristic of the V-shaped flocks
is the high pitched call *kow-kow-kow-kow.*